Machine Learning for Effective Data Mining

Algorithms and Approaches

K. MANOJ A. PETER P. KUMAR

Made with ♥ on the Notion Press Platform

www.notionpress.com

This book is dedicated to all the researchers, scholars, and enthusiasts who are passionate about advancing the field of data mining and machine learning. Your relentless pursuit of knowledge and dedication to pushing the boundaries of what is possible inspire us all.

May this book serve as a valuable resource in your quest for innovation and discovery.

Contents

About the Authors

Dr. K. MANOJ is an Assistant Professor of Statistics at Manonmaniam Sundaranar University in Tamil Nadu, India. With six years of teaching experience and ten years of academic research expertise, he is a prominent figure in the field. Dr. Manoj's research focuses on Data Mining, Outlier Analysis, Time Series, Robust Regression, and Multivariate Analysis. His contributions to the field are notable, with one book and two chapters in an edited volume, as well as 15 research papers published in prestigious international and national journals and proceedings. He has also presented 14 papers at conferences both nationally and internationally. Dr. Manoj is an active member of several esteemed organizations, including the International Society for Clinical Biostatistics (ISCB), the International Association of Engineers (IAENG), the Foundation for Open Access Statistics (FOAS), and the Internet Society (ISOC). Additionally, he is a life member of the Indian Society for Probability and Statistics (ISPS). Dr. Manoj's dedication to advancing statistical knowledge and fostering collaboration within the academic community is evident in his extensive contributions. Through his teaching, research, and active involvement in professional organizations, he continues to make a significant impact in the field of Statistics.

Mr. A. PETER is a Research Scholar in the Department of Statistics at Manonmaniam Sundaranar University, Tirunelveli. He has made significant contributions to his field, with the publication of three research articles in international journals. Additionally, he has actively participated and presented four papers at international conferences. Mr. Peter has also attended numerous workshops, conferences, seminars, and webinars at both the national and international levels, further enriching his knowledge and expertise. He is a member of professional bodies such as IAENG (International Association of Engineers) and ISOC (Internet Society), demonstrating his commitment to professional engagement and networking within his field.

Dr. P. KUMAR received the Master of Science (M.Sc.) degree in Information Technology in 2006, from Alagappa University, Karaikudi, Tamil Nadu, India, Master of Technology (M.Tech.,) degree in Computer and in 2008, Doctor of Philosophy (Ph.D.) in Information Technology-Computer Science and Engineering in 2012 from Manonmaniam Sundaranar University, Abhishekapatti, Tirunelveli, Tamil Nadu, India and Master of Business Administration (M.B.A.) degree in Systems from Alagappa University, Karaikudi, Tamil Nadu, India in 2018. He has 15 years of Teaching / Research experience, currently he is serving as an Associate Professor in the Department of Information Technology and Engineering, Manonmaniam Sundaranar University, Abhishekapatti, Tirunelveli, Tamil Nadu, India. He has published around 125 journal articles /proceedings/books and has produced 08 Ph.D. Scholars. His current research interests include Signal and Image Processing, Artificial Intelligence, Visual Perception, Cyber Security, Computer Networks, Pattern Recognition, Data Analytics, Machine Learning and Deep Learning.

Preface

Welcome to "Machine Learning for Effective Data Mining: Algorithms and Approaches." In this book, we delve into the exciting realm where machine learning intersects with data mining, combining the power of both fields to extract valuable insights and knowledge from complex datasets.

In today's data-driven era, organizations across industries are grappling with the challenges of managing and deriving meaningful information from vast amounts of data. Data mining has long been recognized as a crucial discipline for uncovering patterns, relationships, and actionable intelligence hidden within these expansive datasets. However, the ever-growing scale and complexity of data necessitate advanced techniques to harness its true potential.

Machine learning provides a transformative framework that enables computers to learn from data and make predictions or decisions without explicit programming. By leveraging machine learning algorithms and approaches, we can enhance the effectiveness of data mining, enabling us to extract more accurate, relevant, and actionable insights.

This book serves as a comprehensive guide, equipping readers with the knowledge and tools needed to navigate the intersection of machine learning and data mining. Whether you are a student, a data scientist, or a seasoned professional, the content presented here will enhance your understanding and practical skills in applying machine learning to solve complex data mining problems.

Throughout the chapters, we explore a wide array of machine learning algorithms and approaches tailored specifically for data mining tasks. From classic algorithms such as decision trees, support vector machines, and neural networks, to more recent advancements in deep learning, ensemble methods, and dimensionality reduction techniques, we cover a broad spectrum of techniques that empower you to extract insights effectively.

Moreover, we delve into the critical stages of the data mining process, including data pre-processing, feature selection, model evaluation, and result interpretation. Real-world case studies and examples are incorporated throughout the book to illustrate the practical application of machine learning techniques in data mining.

We would like to express our sincere gratitude to the researchers, practitioners, and educators who have contributed to the vast body of knowledge upon which this book is built. Their ground-breaking work has paved the way for the application of machine learning in data mining and has inspired the content and structure of this guide.

Our hope is that "Machine Learning for Effective Data Mining: Algorithms and Approaches" serves as a valuable resource, empowering you to extract actionable insights from your data and make informed decisions. As the field of machine learning and data mining continues to evolve, may this book be a catalyst for your ongoing exploration and growth, inspiring you to push the boundaries of knowledge extraction from data.

Happy reading and may your journey into the fascinating world of machine learning in data mining be fruitful!

K. MANOJ; A. PETER ; P. KUMAR

25.05.2023

Acknowledgments

Writing a book of this nature involves the collaboration, support, and contributions of many individuals. We would like to express our heartfelt gratitude to all those who have played a part in the creation of "Machine Learning for Effective Data Mining: Algorithms and Approaches."

First and foremost, we extend our deepest appreciation to our families and loved ones for their unwavering support and understanding throughout this endeavour. Their encouragement and belief in us have been invaluable, providing the foundation on which we built this book.

We extend our heartfelt gratitude to Senior Professor Dr. K. Senthamarai Kannan from the Department of Statistics at Manonmaniam Sundaranar University, Tirunelveli, Tamil Nadu. His unwavering support, guidance, and motivation have been instrumental in the successful completion of this book. We are truly indebted to him for his invaluable assistance throughout the entire journey. His expertise and mentorship have significantly enriched the content and quality of this publication.

We are deeply indebted to the esteemed professors who have contributed significantly to this book. Firstly, we extend our sincere gratitude to Dr. A. Loganathan (retired) from the Department of Statistics at Manonmaniam Sundaranar University, Tirunelveli. His valuable insights and discussions have greatly enriched the content of this publication.

We would also like to express our heartfelt appreciation to Dr. A. Rajarathinam, Professor and Head of the Department of Statistics, as well as Dr. P. Arumugam, Professor, and Assistant Professors Dr. R. Sasikumar and Dr. V. Deneshkumar, for their extensive discussions and contributions that have played a crucial role in shaping this book. Their expertise and valuable input have added depth and clarity to the subject matter.

We express our heartfelt gratitude to all the research scholars and students in our department for their valuable contributions and support. Additionally, we extend our special thanks to the office staff members, Mr. A. Srinivasan and Mr. M. Murugesan, for their kind and supportive efforts throughout the process.

While we have made every effort to acknowledge all individuals who have played a part in this book's creation, we apologize if we have inadvertently omitted anyone. Please know that your contributions are deeply appreciated.

Writing this book has been a rewarding and humbling experience. We hope that "Machine Learning for Effective Data Mining: Algorithms and Approaches" serves as a valuable resource, inspiring readers to explore the vast potential of machine learning in the realm of data mining.

Thank you.

K. MANOJ; A. PETER; P. KUMAR

Prologue/Introduction

Data Mining and Machine Learning: Unleashing the Power of Data

In today's data-driven world, the vast amount of information generated has become a valuable asset waiting to be unlocked. Data mining and machine learning are two intertwined fields that harness the power of data to extract meaningful insights and make informed decisions. From uncovering hidden patterns to predicting future trends, these disciplines have revolutionized industries and transformed the way we approach problem-solving.

Data mining, at its core, is the process of discovering patterns, relationships, and valuable information from large datasets. It involves the application of various techniques, such as statistical analysis, machine learning algorithms, and pattern recognition, to identify actionable insights. By sifting through vast amounts of data, data mining allows us to uncover hidden gems that can drive business strategies, improve decision-making, and gain a competitive edge.

Machine learning, on the other hand, is a subset of artificial intelligence that focuses on developing algorithms and models that enable computers to learn and make predictions or decisions without explicit programming. By analyzing patterns and examples within data, machine learning algorithms can automatically identify and adapt to underlying patterns, ultimately improving their performance over time. This powerful capability has led to breakthroughs in areas such as image recognition, natural language processing, and predictive analytics.

Throughout this book, we will delve into the fascinating world of data mining and machine learning, exploring their fundamental principles, methodologies, and applications. We will discuss various data mining techniques, including association rules, clustering, classification, and outlier detection, as well as delve into different types of machine learning algorithms, such as supervised learning, unsupervised learning, and reinforcement learning.

Moreover, we will explore real-world case studies and examples that highlight the practical applications of data mining and machine learning across various industries, including finance, healthcare, marketing, and social media. From fraud detection to personalized recommendations, from predictive maintenance to customer segmentation, the potential applications of these fields are vast and continuously expanding.

By understanding the principles and techniques of data mining and machine learning, readers will gain the necessary knowledge and skills to extract valuable insights from data, develop predictive models, and make data-driven decisions. Whether you are a student, researcher, or industry professional, this book aims to provide a comprehensive and practical guide to harnessing the power of data and unleashing the potential of data mining and machine learning.

Join us on this exciting journey as we unlock the hidden treasures buried within data and harness the immense potential of data mining and machine learning. Let's embark on a quest to unravel the mysteries of data and transform it into actionable knowledge for a better tomorrow.

1. Data Mining

What is Data Mining?

Data mining is the practice of automatically searching large stores of data to discover patterns and trends that go beyond simple analysis. Data mining uses sophisticated mathematical algorithms to segment the data and evaluate the probability of future events. Data mining is also known as Knowledge Discovery in Data (KDD).

Data mining refers to extracting or mining knowledge from large databases. Data mining and knowledge discovery in the databases is a new interdisciplinary field, merging ideas from statistics, machine learning, databases and parallel computing (Manoj2015).

Some of the definitions of data mining are:

Definition 1.1. Data mining (sometimes called data or knowledge discovery) is the process of analyzing data from different perspectives and summarizing it into useful information.

Definition 1.2. Data mining is the non-trivial extraction of implicit, preciously unknown and potentially useful information from the data.

Definition 1.3. Data mining is the search for the relationships and global patterns that exist in large databases but are hidden among vast amounts of data.

The Knowledge Discovery Data Process

Data mining is the process of discovering interesting patterns from massive amounts of data (Han2022). As knowledge discovery process, it typically involves data cleaning, data integration, data selection, data transformation, pattern discovery, pattern evaluation, and knowledge presentation.

The knowledge discovery process is shown in figure 1.1 as an iterative sequence of the following steps.

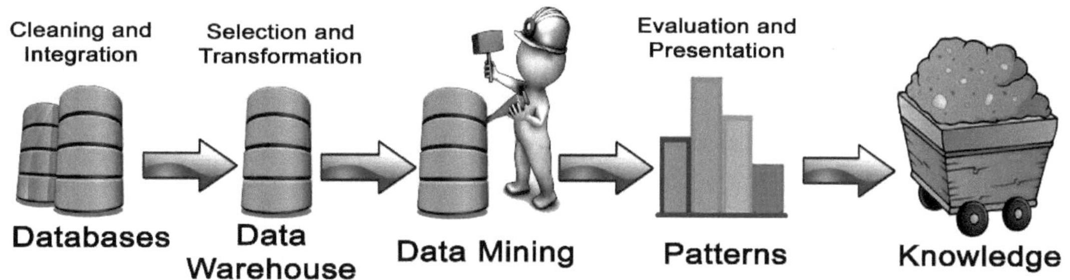

Figure 1.1: Data Mining steps for Knowledge Discovery

- **Data cleaning** to remove noise and inconsistent data
- **Data integration** where multiple data sources may be combined
- **Data selection** where data relevant to the analysis task are retrieved from the database

- **Data transformation** where data are transformed and consolidated into forms appropriate for mining by performing summary or aggregation operations
- **Data mining** an essential process where intelligent methods are applied to extract data patterns
- **Pattern evaluation** to identify the truly interesting patterns representing knowledge based on interesting measures
- **Knowledge presentation** were visualization and knowledge representation techniques are used to present mined knowledge to users

Data Mining and Statistics

Data mining and statistics are two closely related disciplines that play a crucial role in extracting valuable insights and patterns from data. While they share some similarities, they also have distinct characteristics and purposes.

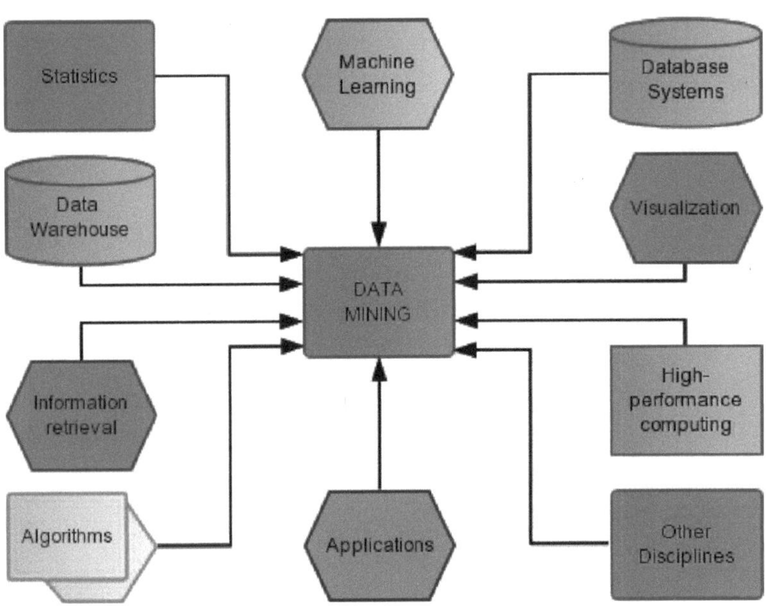

Figure 1.2: Data Mining Disciplines

Data mining refers to the process of discovering patterns, relationships, and knowledge from large datasets. It involves employing various techniques, such as machine learning, artificial intelligence, and statistical analysis, to uncover hidden patterns and make predictions or decisions based on the data. Data mining aims to extract meaningful information and insights from vast amounts of data, often stored in databases or data warehouses. It involves tasks such as data pre-processing, data transformation, pattern discovery, and result evaluation. Data mining techniques can be applied in diverse fields, including business, healthcare, finance, and marketing, to identify trends, make predictions, and support decision-making processes.

On the other hand, statistics is a branch of mathematics that focuses on collecting, analyzing, interpreting, and presenting data. Statistics provides tools and techniques for summarizing data, performing statistical inference, and making probabilistic predictions. It involves methods such as sampling, hypothesis testing, regression analysis, and probability theory. Statistics aims to draw reliable conclusions and make inferences about a population based on sample data. It provides a framework for quantifying uncertainty, estimating parameters, and evaluating the significance of relationships between variables.

While data mining and statistics share common goals of extracting knowledge from data, they differ in their approaches and emphasis. Data mining is more focused on discovering hidden patterns and relationships in large datasets, often using automated techniques and machine learning algorithms. It leverages computational power and advanced analytics to handle vast amounts of data and uncover insights that may not be apparent through traditional statistical analysis. Statistics, on the other hand, emphasizes inference, hypothesis testing, and parameter estimation. It often deals with smaller sample sizes and aims to draw conclusions about the entire population based on the available data.

In practice, data mining and statistics often complement each other. Statistics provides a solid foundation for data analysis, hypothesis testing, and drawing reliable conclusions. Data mining techniques, on the other hand, enhance the analysis by uncovering complex patterns, relationships, and trends that may not be readily apparent. By combining the strengths of both disciplines, organizations can gain a deeper understanding of their data and make more informed decisions.

Applying statistical methods in data mining is far from trivial. Often, a serious challenge is how to scale up a statistical method over a large data set. Many statistical methods have high complexity in computation. When such methods are applied on large data sets that are also distributed on multiple logical or physical sites, algorithms should be carefully designed and tuned to reduce the computational cost.

This challenge becomes even tougher for online applications, such as online query suggestions in search engines, where data mining is required to continuously handle fast, real-time data streams. Traditional statistical methods, in general, require a great deal of user interaction in order to validate the correctness of a model. As a result, statistical methods can be difficult to automate. Moreover, statistical methods typically do not scale well to very large data sets. Statistical methods rely on testing hypotheses or finding correlations based on smaller, representative samples of a larger population.

Data mining methods are suitable for large data sets and can be more readily automated. In fact, data mining algorithms often require large data sets for the creation of quality models.

In this chapter contains a brief introduction about the data mining and its process with data mining and statistical methods and tools required for the data cleaning, data integration, data selection, data transformation, pattern discovery, pattern evaluation, and knowledge presentation.

2. Machine Learning

The goal of machine learning is to build computer systems that can adapt and learn from their experience.

- Tom Mitchell

First coined by Arthur Samuel, machine learning can be defined as the field of computer science that gives computers the ability to learn without being explicitly programmed (Samuel1988). Emerging from the study of pattern recognition and computational learning theory in artificial intelligence, machine learning algorithms are developed that can learn from a large amount of data and make predictions on the data (Kohavi1998). Machine learning investigates how computers can learn (or improve their performance) based on data.

A main research area is for computer programs to automatically learn to recognize complex patterns and make intelligent decisions based on data. For example, a typical machine learning problem is to program a computer so that it can automatically recognize handwritten postal codes on mail after learning from a set of examples. Machine learning is a fast-growing discipline. Here, we illustrate classic problems in machine learning that are highly related to data mining.

General classes of machine learning methods include (Goecks2020):

a) supervised learning in which data groups are associated with a specific outcome; categorical data (e.g., disease vs. normal) rely on classification methods whereas continuous values (e.g., strength of response to therapy) are used in regression methods,

b) unsupervised or semi-supervised methods to cluster data into discrete groups that can then be manually labeled and associated with outcome,

c) ensemble learning, where results from multiple computational models are combined to produce a final prediction, can lead to more accurate predictions by enabling models to generalize to new data better

d) deep learning, which uses artificial neural networks, a formalization modelled on the human brain, to recognize patterns or associations in the data, is especially useful when working with unstructured data such as images, speech, and text and

e) Bayesian learning, in which prior knowledge is encoded into the learning process, is especially useful in data-poor situations.

Supervised Learning

Supervised learning is basically a synonym for classification. The supervision in the learning comes from the labeled examples in the training data set. For example, in the postal code recognition problem, a set of handwritten postal code images and their corresponding machine-readable translations are used as the training examples, which supervise the learning of the classification model.

Unsupervised learning is essentially a synonym for clustering. The learning process is unsupervised since the input examples are not class labeled. Typically, we may use clustering to discover classes within the data. For example, an unsupervised learning method can take, as input, a set of images of handwritten digits. Suppose that it finds 10 clusters of data. These clusters may correspond to the 10 distinct digits of 0 to 9, respectively. However, since the training data are not labeled, the learned model cannot tell us the semantic meaning of the clusters found.

Semi-supervised learning is a class of machine learning techniques that make use of both labeled and unlabeled examples when learning a model. In one approach, labeled examples are used to learn class models and unlabeled examples are used to refine the boundaries between classes. For a two-class problem, we can think of the set of examples belonging to one class as the positive examples and those belonging to the other class as the negative examples. If we do not consider the unlabeled examples, the dashed line is the decision boundary that best partitions the positive examples from the negative examples. Using the unlabeled examples, we can refine the decision boundary to the solid line. Moreover, we can detect that the two positive examples at the top right corner, though labeled, are likely noise or outliers.

Active learning Active learning is a machine learning approach that lets users play an active role in the learning process. An active learning approach can ask a user (e.g., a domain expert) to label an example, which may be from a set of unlabeled examples or synthesized by the learning program. The goal is to optimize the model quality by actively acquiring knowledge from human users, given a constraint on how many examples they can be asked to label. There are many similarities between data mining and machine learning. For classification and clustering tasks, machine learning research often focuses on the accuracy of the model. In addition to accuracy, data mining research places strong emphasis on the efficiency and scalability of mining methods on large data sets, as well as on ways to handle complex types of data and explore new, alternative methods.

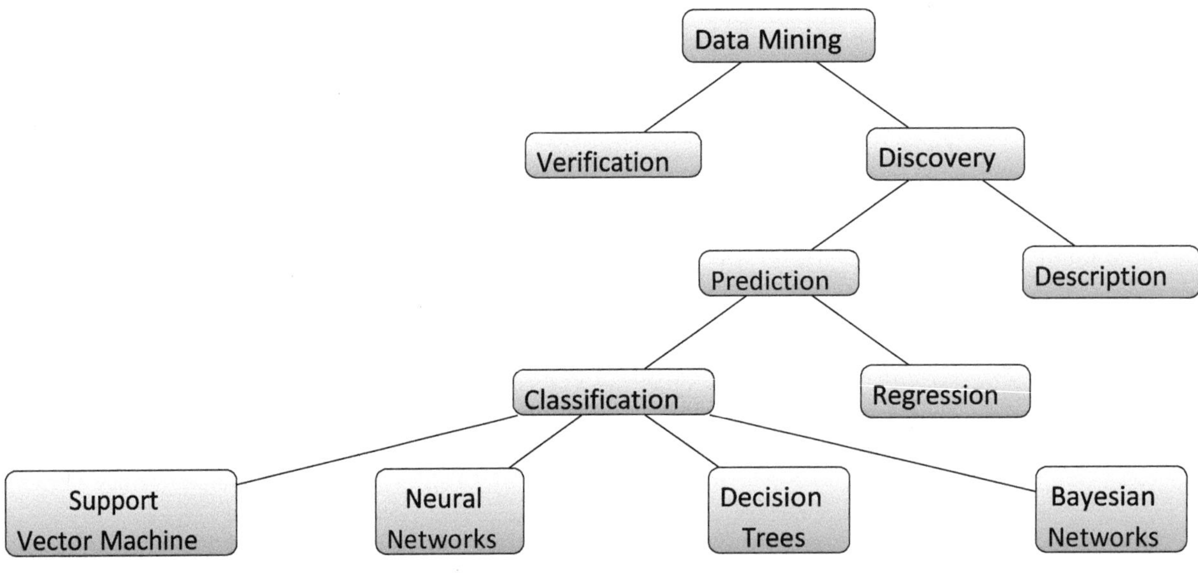

Figure 2.1: Classification of Data Mining

Data Mining and Machine Learning

In this present era, current generation are highly influenced by the conception, named as “Digitalization”. This insight of digitalization is playing highly important role in every sector of the banking, financial, insurance and other economic sectors. Normally, moving towards to digitalization is important for the Indian banking sector as it plays a most significant role in financial inclusion, which is mostly disturbed for offering the best services to customers with a prospect for gaining more in the future. Generally, online banking is a familiar standard for transferring currency from one account to another account. Online banking is getting fame gradually, which increases online transaction with enhanced facilities in various domains such as insurance premium, online reservation for buses, railways, utilities bill payments, such as electricity, house and water taxes, online shopping and so on. Online banking performances are continually increasing. On the other hand, this development has also one major drawback such as an increase in fraudulent activities. Online banking is also named e-banking or internet banking and it developed quickly in precedent years. In the recent days, internet banking is an essential service even for the common people.

Electronic banking is a novel banking service, which permits people for interacting with their banking accounts through the internet. Electronic banking provides various banking services, such as Automatic Teller Machine (ATM) services, Electronic Transfer of Funds (EFT), direct deposit Automatic Bill Payment (ABP), and so on. Moreover, this method is a better advantageous medium for the financial association. However, this banking method is inexpensive, while compared with the customary banking method and it provides custom comfort and flexibility. This enhanced development of the online banking system experienced various challenges because of risk and attacks of fraud data settlement. In this modern world, hackers utilize various approaches for violating the security of e-banking. Online application providers in business-to-business segments and business-to-customer segments are increased tremendously, consequently the fraudulent activities and attacks also increased proportionally. In this context, there is an essential need of strong authentication strategies during online transactions. With the advancement and availability of information and communication systems raised the demand for numerous advanced techniques to facilitate Security of cryptographic systems in more sophisticated manner.

Database Systems and Data Warehouses

Database systems research focuses on the creation, maintenance, and use of databases for organizations and end-users. Particularly, database systems researchers have established highly recognized principles in data models, query languages, query processing and optimization methods, data storage, and indexing and accessing methods. Database systems are often well known for their high scalability in processing very large, relatively structured data sets.

Many data mining tasks need to handle large data sets or even real-time, fast streaming data. Therefore, data mining can make good use of scalable database technologies to achieve high efficiency and scalability on large data sets. Moreover, data mining tasks can be used to extend the capability of existing database systems to satisfy advanced users' sophisticated data analysis requirements.

Recent database systems have built systematic data analysis capabilities on database data using data warehousing and data mining facilities. A data warehouse integrates data originating from multiple sources and various time frames. It consolidates data in multidimensional space to form partially materialized data cubes. The data cube model not only facilitates OLAP in multidimensional databases but also promotes multidimensional data mining.

Bayes Classification Methods

Bayes' theorem is named after Thomas Bayes, a nonconformist English clergyman who did early work in probability and decision theory during the 18th century. Let X be a data tuple. In Bayesian terms, X is considered "evidence." As usual, it is described by measurements made on a set of n attributes. Let H be some hypothesis such as that the data tuple X belongs to a specified class C. For classification problems, we want to determine P(H|X), the probability that the hypothesis H holds given the "evidence" or observed data tuple X. In other words, we are looking for the probability that tuple X belongs to class C, given that we know the attribute description of X (Han2022).

P(H|X) is the posterior probability, or a posteriori probability, of H conditioned on X. For example, suppose our world of data tuples is confined to customers described by the attributes age and income, respectively, and that X is a 35-year-old customer with an income of $40,000. Suppose that H is the hypothesis that our customer will buy a computer. Then P(H|X) reflects the probability that customer X will buy a computer given that we know the customer's age and income.

In contrast, P(H) is the prior probability, or a priori probability, of H. For our example, this is the probability that any given customer will buy a computer, regardless of age, income, or any other information, for that matter. The posterior probability, P(H|X), is based on more information (e.g., customer information) than the prior probability, P(H), which is independent of X.

Similarly, (X|H) is the posterior probability of X conditioned on H. That is, it is the probability that a customer, X, is 35 years old and earns $40,000, given that we know the customer will buy a computer. P(X) is the prior probability of X. Using our example, it is the probability that a person from our set of customers is 35 years old and earns $40,000. "How are these probabilities estimated?" P(H), P(X|H), and P(X) may be estimated from the given data, as we shall see next. Bayes' theorem is useful in that it provides a way of calculating the posterior probability, P(H|X), from P(H), P(X|H), and P(X). Bayes' theorem is

$$P(X|H) = \frac{P(X|H)P(H)}{P(X)}$$

Now that we have that out of the way, in the next section, we will look at how Bayes' theorem is used in the naïve Bayesian classifier.

Naive Bayes classifier

The Naive Bayes classifier (ShalevShwartz2014) is a classical demonstration of how generative assumptions and parameter estimations simplify the learning process.

Consider the problem of predicting a label y ∈ {0, 1} on the basis of a vector of features $x = (x_1, \dots, x_d)$, where we assume that each x_i is in {0,1}. Recall that the Bayes optimal classifier is

$$h_{\text{bayes}}(x) = \text{argmax}P\ [(Y = y|X = x)]\ \ y \in\{0,1\}$$

To describe the probability function P[Y = y | X = x] we need 2d parameters, each of which corresponds to

P[Y = 1 | X = x] for a certain value of $x \in \{0,1\}^d$. This implies that the number of examples we need grows exponentially with the number of features.

In the Naive Bayes approach, we make the (rather naive) generative assumption that given the label, the features are independent of each other. That is,

$$\rho\ [X = x\ |Y = y] = \prod \rho\ [X_i = x_i\ |Y = y].$$

With this assumption and using Bayes' rule, the Bayes optimal classifier can be further simplified:

$$h_{\text{bayes}}(x) = \text{argmax}\ \rho\ [(Y = y|X = x)]\ \ y \in\{0,1\}$$

That is, now the number of parameters we need to estimate is only 2d+1. Here, the generative assumption we made reduced significantly the number of parameters we need to learn. When we also estimate the parameters using the maximum likelihood principle, the resulting classifier is called the Naive Bayes classifier.

Long Short-Term Memory (LSTM)

LSTM is a kind of recurrent neural network (Introduced by Hochreiter1997) that solves the vanishing gradient problem in vanilla RNNs with additional cells, input and output gates. Intuitively, vanishing gradients are resolved by additional additive elements and forget gate activations, allowing the gradients to flow through the network without rapidly vanishing. Let's say while watching a video you remember the previous scene or while reading a book you know what happened in the earlier chapter. Similarly, RNNs work, they remember the previous information and use it for processing the current input. The shortcoming of RNN is, they cannot remember Long-term dependencies due to vanishing gradient. LSTMs are explicitly designed to avoid long-term dependency problems.

A solution to this problem is to capture the necessary complexity in the form of other matrices called gates. The LSTM introduces three types of gates—input gate, output gate, and forget gate. The input gate combines the input and updates the h vector, the output gate combines the current and previous h vectors and the forget gate prevents the current h vector from updates to the given RNN unit (Yeturu2020).

LSTM Architecture

At a high-level LSTM works very much like an RNN cell. Here is the internal functioning of the LSTM network. The LSTM consists of three parts, as shown in Figure 1.4 and each part performs an individual function.

The first part chooses whether the information coming from the previous timestamp is to be remembered or is irrelevant and can be forgotten. In the second part, the cell tries to learn new information from the input to this cell. At last, in the third part, the cell passes the updated information from the current timestamp to the next timestamp. These three parts of an LSTM cell are known as gates. The first part is called Forget gate, the second part is known as the Input gate and the last one is the Output gate shown in Figure 2.2.

A simple RNN, an LSTM also has a hidden state where H(t −1) represents the hidden state of the previous timestamp and Ht is the hidden state of the current timestamp. In addition to that LSTM also have a cell state represented by C(t −1) and C(t) for previous and current timestamp respectively.

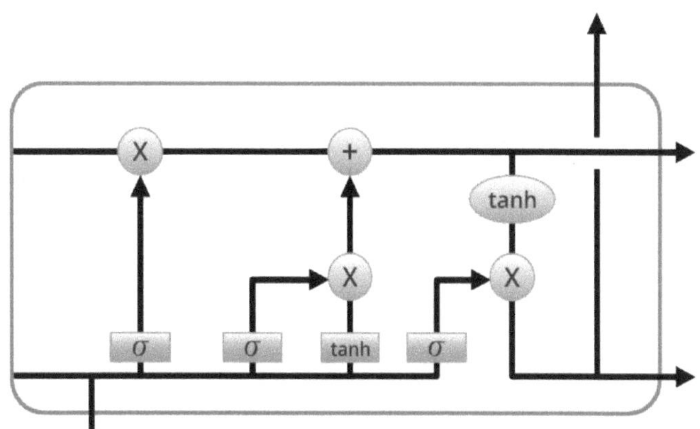

Image Source: www.geeksforgeeks.org

Figure 2.2: Forget Gate of LSTM

Forget Gate

In a cell of the LSTM network, the first step is to decide whether we should keep the information from the previous timestamp or forget it. Here is the equation for forget gate.

Forget Gate: $f_t = \sigma(x_t \times U_f \times H_{t-1} \times W_f)$

Let's try to understand the equation, here

X_t: input to the current timestamp.

U_f : weight associated with the input

H_{t-1}: The hidden state of the previous timestamp

W_f : It is the weight matrix associated with hidden state

Later, a sigmoid function is applied over it. That will make f_t a number between 0 and 1. This f_t is later multiplied with the cell state of the previous timestamp as shown below.

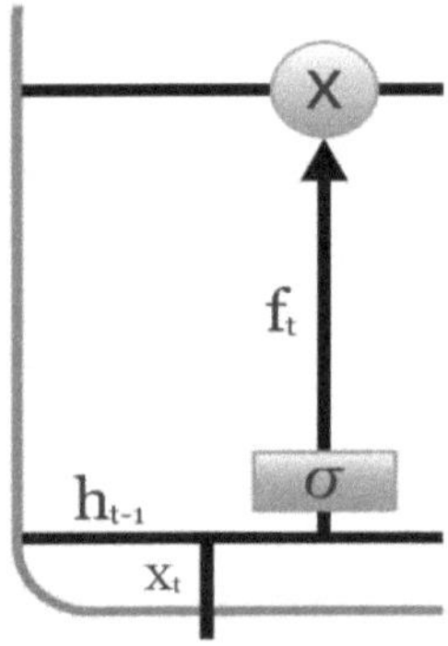

Image Source: www.geeksforgeeks.org

Figure 2.3: Forget Gate of LSTM

$$C_{t-1} * f_t = 0 \quad ...if\ f_t = 0 (forget\ everything)$$

$$C_{t-1} * f_t = C_{t-1} \quad ...if\ f_t = 1 (forget\ nothing)$$

If f_t is 0 then the network will forget everything and if the value of f_t is 1 it will forget nothing. Let's get back to our example, the first sentence was talking about Bob and after a full stop, the network will encounter Dan, in an ideal case the network should forget about Bob.

Input Gate

The addition of useful information to the cell state is done by the input gate. First, the information is regulated using the sigmoid function and filter the values to be remembered similar to the forget gate using inputs ht−1 and xt. Then, a vector is created using tanh function that gives an output from −1 to +1, which contains all the possible values from ht−1 and xt. At last, the values of the vector and the regulated values are multiplied to obtain the useful information

Input gate is used to quantify the importance of the new information carried by the input. Here is the equation of the input gate

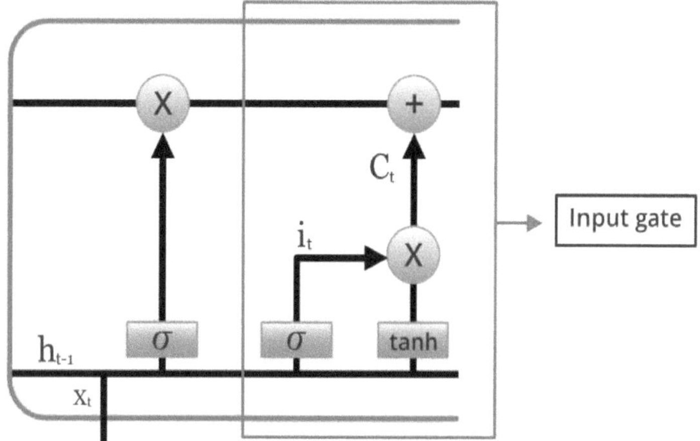

Image Source: www.geeksforgeeks.org

Figure 2.4: Input Gate for LSTM

Input Gate: $i_t = \sigma(x_t * U_i + H_{t-1} * W_i)$

Here,

X_t: Input at the current timestamp t

U_i: weight matrix of input

H_{t-1}: A hidden state at the previous timestamp

W_i: Weight matrix of input associated with hidden state

Again, we have applied sigmoid function over it. As a result, the value of I at timestamp t will be between 0 and 1.

$$N_t = \tanh(x_t * U_c + H_{t-1} * W_c)$$

Now the new information that needed to be passed to the cell state is a function of a hidden state at the previous timestamp t − 1 and input xat timestamp t. The activation function here is tanh. Due to the tanh function, the value of new information will between−1and 1. If the value is of Nt is negative the information is subtracted from the cell state and if the value is positive the information is added to the cell state at the current timestamp.

However, the N_t won't be added directly to the cell state. Here comes the updated equation

$$C_t = f_t * C_{t-1} + i_t * N_t \text{ (updating cell state)}$$

Here, C_{t-1} is the cell state at the current timestamp and others are the values we have calculated previously

Output Gate

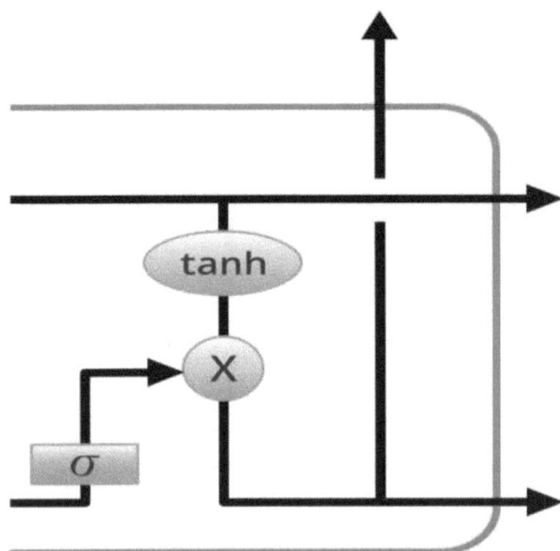

Image Source: www.geeksforgeeks.org

Figure 2.5: Output Gate for LSTM

The task of extracting useful information from the current cell state to be presented as output is done by the output gate. First, a vector is generated by applying tanh function on the cell. Then, the information is regulated using the sigmoid function and filter by the values to be remembered using inputs ht−1 and xt. At last, the values of the vector and the regulated values are multiplied to be sent as an output and input to the next cell.

Here is the equation of the Output gate, which is pretty similar to the two previous gates.

$$Output\ Gate : O_t = \sigma(x_t * U_o + H_{t-1} * W_o)$$

Its value will also lie between 0 and 1 because of this sigmoid function. Now to calculate the current hidden state we will use O_t and tanh of the updated cell state. As shown below.

$$H_t = o_t * \tanh(C_t)$$

It turns out that the hidden state is a function of Long term memory (C_t) and the current output. If you need to take the output of the current timestamp just apply the SoftMax activation on hidden state H_t.

$$\text{Output} = soft\ \max(H_t)$$

This chapter presents a brief information about the various research works carried out earlier in the context Credit Card Fraud issues of with respect to various Machine Learning techniques including Artificial Neural Network, Supervised and Unsupervised Machine Learning Techniques.

******

3. Artificial Neural Network

Introduction

An artificial neural network is a model of computation inspired by the structure of neural networks in the brain. In simplified models of the brain, it consists of a large number of basic computing devices (neurons) that are connected to each other in a complex communication network, through which the brain is able to carry out highly complex computations. An Artificial Neural Network consists of nodes, also called neurons, weighted connections between these neurons that can be adapted during the learning process of the network and an activation function that defines the output value of each node depending on its input values.

Every neural network consists of different layers. The input layer receives information from external sources, such as attribute values of the corresponding data entry, the output layer produces the output of the network and hidden layers connect the input and the output layer with one another. The input value of each node in every layer is calculated by the sum of all incoming nodes multiplied with the respective weight of the interconnection between the nodes (Erb1993). Furthermore, neural networks can be divided into two main types (Zhang2004):

Feed forward Networks are defined as all networks that do not gain feedback from the network itself. This means that the input data flows in one direction, from the input nodes through 0 to n hidden nodes to the output nodes. There is no information given backwards to readapt the system. Recurrent Networks are defined as all networks that contain a feedback option and therefore are able to reuse data from later stages for the learning process in earlier stages.

The output value of each node is calculated by using all input values on a predefined function that is the same for every node in the network. The most commonly used function is the sigmoid function oj, which is defined as follows (Erb1993):

Where ij is the sum of the input nodes of j. According to Erb, the two main advantages of this function are its normalization to values between 0 and 1 and its nonlinear nature, which results in easier rapid network learning and prevention of overload and domination effects. A domination effect occurs, when a single or a few attributes get a very high influence on the predicted target attribute, rendering other attributes meaningless and therefore dominating them (Erb1993).

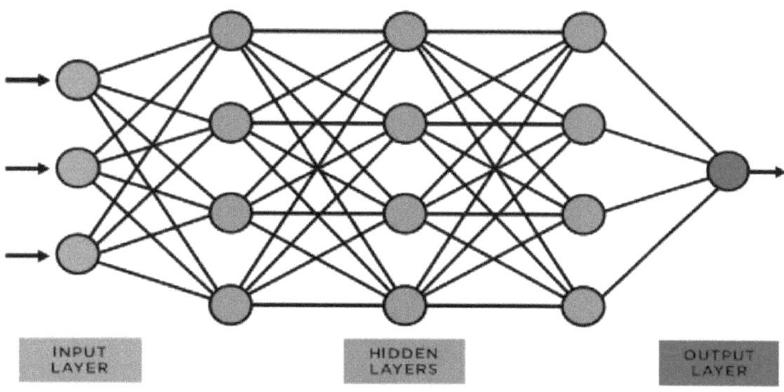

Image Source: www.tibco.com

Figure 3.1: Neural Network with three input nodes

Neural Network Architecture

Input Nodes (input layer): No computation is done here within this layer; they just pass the information to the next layer (hidden layer most of the time). A block of nodes is also called layer.

Hidden nodes (hidden layer): In Hidden layers is where intermediate processing or computation is done, they perform computations and then transfer the weights (signals or information) from the input layer to the following layer (another hidden layer or to the output layer).

Output Nodes (output layer): Here we finally use an activation function that maps to the desired output format (e.g., SoftMax for classification).

Connections and weights: The network consist of connections, each connection transferring the output of a neuron i to the input of a neuron j. In this sense i is the predecessor of j and j is the successor of i, each connection is assigned a weight W_{ij}.

Activation function: The activation function of a node defines the output of that node given an input or set of inputs. A standard computer chip circuit can be seen as a digital network of activation functions that can be "ON" (1) or "OFF" (0), depending on input. This is similar to the behavior of the linear perceptron in neural networks. However, it is the nonlinear activation function that allows such networks to compute nontrivial problems using only a small number of nodes. In artificial neural networks this function is also called the transfer function.

Learning rule: The learning rule is a rule or an algorithm which modifies the parameters of the neural network, in order for a given input to the network to produce a favored output. This learning process typically amounts to modifying the weights and thresholds.

Types of Neural Networks

There are many classes of neural networks and these classes also have sub-classes, here I will list the most used ones and make things simple to move on in this journey to learn neural networks.

Feed forward Neural Network

A feed forward neural network is an artificial neural network where connections between the units do not form a cycle. In this network, the information moves in only one direction, forward, from the input nodes, through the hidden nodes (if any) and to the output nodes. There are no cycles or loops in the network. We can distinguish two types of feed forward neural networks:

Single-layer Perceptron

This is the simplest feed forward neural Network and does not contain any hidden layer, which means it only consists of a single layer of output nodes. This is said to be single because when we count the layers, we do not include the input layer, the reason for that is because at the input layer no computations is done, the inputs are fed directly to the outputs via a series of weights (Figure 3.2).

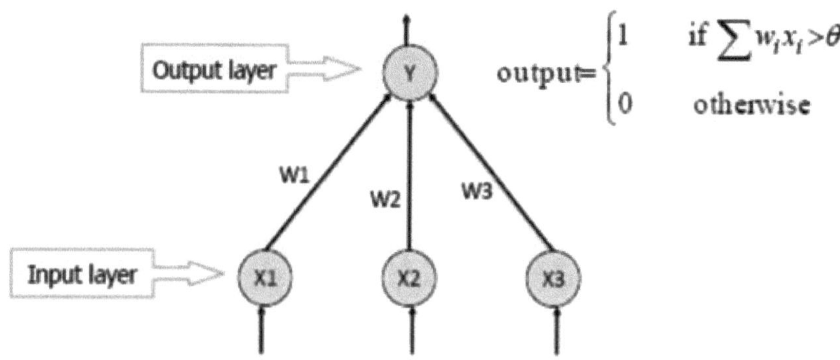

Figure 3.2: Example of Single-layer Perceptron

Multi-layer perceptron (MLP)

This class of networks consists of multiple layers of computational units, usually interconnected in a feed-forward way. Each neuron in one layer has directed connections to the neurons of the subsequent layer. In many applications the units of these networks apply a sigmoid function as an activation function. MLP are very more useful and one good reason is that, they are able to learn non-linear representations (most of the cases the data presented to us is not linearly separable)

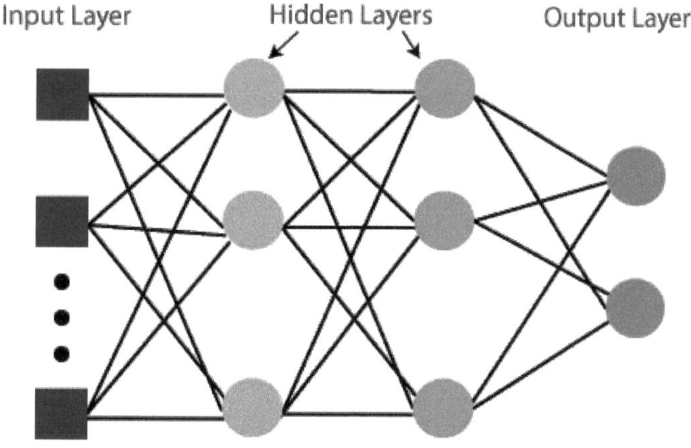

Figure 3.3: Multi-layer Perceptron

Convolutional Neural Network (CNN)

Convolutional Neural Networks are very similar to ordinary Neural Networks, they are made up of neurons that have learnable weights and biases. In convolutional neural network (CNN, or ConvNet or shift invariant or space invariant) the unit connectivity pattern is inspired by the organization of the visual cortex, Units respond to stimuli in a restricted region of space known as the receptive field. Receptive fields partially overlap, over-covering the entire visual field. Unit response can be approximated mathematically by a convolution operation. They are variations of multilayer perceptron's that use minimal pre-processing. Their wide applications is in image and video recognition, recommender systems and natural language processing. CNNs requires large data to train on Figure 3.4.

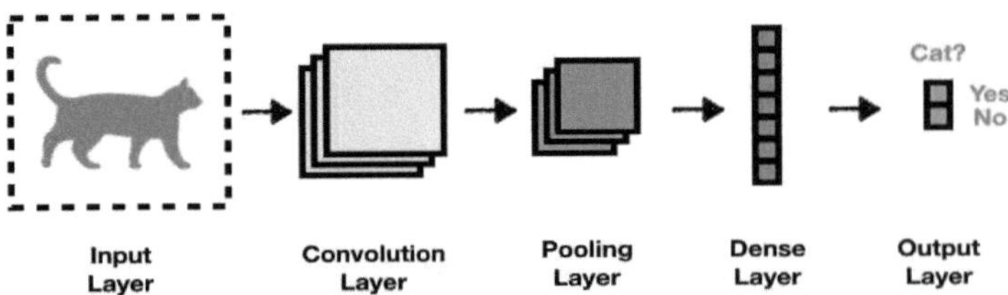

Figure 3.4: Convolutional Neural Network

Recurrent neural networks

In recurrent neural network (RNN), connections between units form a directed cycle (they propagate data forward, but also backwards, from later processing stages to earlier stages). This allows it to exhibit dynamic temporal behaviour. Unlike feed forward neural networks, RNNs can use their internal memory to process arbitrary sequences of inputs. This makes them applicable to tasks such as un-segmented, connected handwriting recognition, speech recognition and other general sequence processors.

Artificial Neural Networks and the Brain

Artificial neural networks doesn't work like our brain, ANN are simple crude comparison, the connections between biological networks are much more complex than those implemented by Artificial neural network architectures, remember, our brain is much more complex and there is more we need to learn from it. There are many things we don't know about our brain and this also makes hard to know how we should model an Artificial Brain to reason at human level. Whenever we train a neural network, we want our model to learn the optimal weights (w) that best predicts the desired outcome (y) given the input signals or information (x).

Banking

The banking segment is the lifeline of various current economies. It is the significant financial pillars of the financial segment, which plays an essential role in economic functioning. Moreover, it is the most significant one for the economic progression of a country, and its financing needs of trade, agriculture, and industry are assembling with a high degree of responsibility and commitment. Therefore, the progression of the country is integrally associated with the expansion of banking. In the current economy, banks are considered not as a trader in money but as leaders of progression. The banking system also plays an imperative task in the mobilization of payment and deposits of credit in several segments of the economy. Normally, the banking structure replicates the economic health of a country. The power of an economy relies on the effectiveness and strength of the financial structure, and it depends on a solvent and sound banking scheme. The sound banking method is effectively organized in dynamic segments and also solvent banking structure guarantees that the bank is proficient to meet its necessities to depositors. The progressing technology in the banking segment has major inferences for banks marketing efforts, particularly in digital banking customer interface. Along with this, digital banking through mobile, internet, and telephone becomes the main method for delivering multi-channel services to customers, and it a challenging one as compared with the traditional banking system. The digital banking system enlarges the customer expectations in which productivity improvement is a significant one.

Normally, the banking segment is the backbone of economic domains and it executes various financial strategies. The alternations of the financial section have a wide impact on the progression of the economy. In modern days, banks are seeking alternative ways of providing and distinguishing various services. In general, retail customers and corporations are not ready to queue in banks, wait on phone calls for fundamental banking services. The corporate and retail customer needs a resource for performing their banking services at any location and time. Plastic money, such as smart cards, debit cards, and credit cards and internet banking contain branch networking, online trading accounts, electronic payment services, telephone banking, mobile applications, online investments, wallet and electronic fund transfers are various modern services of the banking system. Information technology progressions in the banking section have various advantages to transaction and communication for clients. Moreover, this information technology development plays an essential role in the banking services. Internet is a low-cost delivery way for banking products and it permits various entities for reducing their branch networks and rationalizes the number of service employees. Since internet banking is one of the major competitive advantages of financial entity the navigability of the website is a very significant section of the internet banking system. The utilization of banking systems increases every day because of the development in information technology. Apart from this, internet banking is an essential element of recent time banking services.

Digital Banking

Digital banking or an electronic banking is a novel trade, it allows people to interact with their banking accounts over the internet from any remote location. The electronic banking system deals with various expansions, to name a few, client demand for anywhere, anytime services, product time to market essentials, and difficulty of bank office integration problems. The digital banking system permits the customers for accessing their banking account, demand a current account statement, reorder checks, product information, observation of current bank rates, and accessing latest transactions. Along with this, various banks, namely Citibank, Fleet Financial Group, Royal Bank of Canada, Chevy Chase, Bank of America,

Mellon Bank, KeyCorp, Michigan National Bank, Bank One, Bank, Comerica, First Bank Systems, and so on are presently providing these services. The electronic banking system is normally considered as an expansion of present banking system. Moreover, Internet banking is termed as any user with browser and computer can be linked to their bank website for performing various essential banking operations. Besides, the bank has a federal dataset, which is web-enabled in digital banking. Internet banking is a borderless entity, which allows to perform all banking services at anyhow, anytime and everywhere.

In modern days, internet banking is the most advanced technology in the economic section. Internet banking systems enables bank customers for obtaining contact with their accounts and general information on bank services and products. The internet banking system utilizes bank websites without involvement or difficulty of original signatures, faxes, telephone confirmations, and sending letters. Furthermore, internet banking is the type of service in which customers can perform most retail banking services, like inter-account transfers, balance verification, and reporting any issues by means of telecommunication network without leaving their home or present location of the customers. Additionally, it offers a global connection from various positions and it is commonly accessible from every internet- connected computer. Even though, internet banking has various advantages there is a problem, termed as security. Security is a significant one in the electronic banking service. Even though, electronic banking is a modern technology, which has various capacities and also several potential issues, so some users may hesitate to use this type of systems. The number of malicious applications targeting online banking transactions are enlarged significantly in current years. Moreover, there are several digital banking services, like real- time gross settlement, interbank mobile payment system, credit cards, mobile banking, debit cards, national electronic fund transfer, and so on are offered through the banks to its customers.

The digital banking system is utilized by the customers through various handheld devices such as smart phones, tablets and other electronic gadgets. Online banking is referred as the utilization of the internet to perform bank transactions whereas mobile banking is termed as the service of mobile phone for conducting banking services. Furthermore, there is a rapid progression of banking transactions in the modern years. Throughout the worldwide, non- cash transactions are increased about 10.1% in 2016 to 482.6 billion and it is computed to speed up the composite annual progress of 12.7% between 2016 and 2021. However, digital banking fraud is a severe problem in financial crime management for every bank. On the other hand, it leads to more difficult and huge losses because of the development and emergence of complicated online banking fraud, through ghost websites, malware infection, phishing scams, and so on and so forth.

Online electronic banking scheme offers the chance to every person for uncomplicated access to their banking performances. The banking performance contains, money transfer, recovering account balance, recovering account history, etc. various banks permit other services, like compliance of uniform account payment files for bank transactions for third parties, stock market transactions, and so on. Apart from this, e-banking is a condition of innovative and conventional banking activities and products to clients through interactive and electronic communication channels. E-banking system provides customer services, such as payment instructions, credit accounting, account access, electronic fund transfer, and attaining information on financial services and products through electronic channels. Normally, e-banking functionality can be separated into three stages. In the first stage, it contains an information, which only offers openly obtainable information and their significant principles of marketing. In the second level, the system permits to access information of the particular user's and specific services. At last, the most advanced system is employed in the third level, it allows other financial transactions and electronic fund transfer in addition to it permits the users to contribute to transactional services.

Security in Digital Banking

Security is one of the main challenging issues for any digital banking services. In the early days, if a thief wants to steal a person's money, it is a very complex one and it includes numerous risks and dangers. Although, in online banking cybercriminals only require the assured personal information for breaking a person's account and steal their money. Normally, privacy has four main classes, namely bodily privacy, territorial privacy, information privacy, and communication privacy. Internet privacy is mainly information privacy, which means the capability of an individual for controlling information about oneself. Moreover, the offensive of privacy presents, while individuals cannot preserve the extensive degree of control over the individual information and its utilization. Besides, information security includes major three sections, such as availability, integrity, and confidentiality. The Certified Internal Auditor (CIA) is generally utilized benchmark for assessment of information system security in an e-commerce environment. These three elements of security may affect through purposeful human causes, technical problems, natural occurrence, accidental, and so on. Confidentiality is termed as the limitations of information access and confession for official users and avoiding access by unauthorized users. Additionally, confidentiality is a declaration in which information is only shared between authorized organizations and persons. Authentication techniques, such as passwords and user identifications are utilized for identifying users and it helps to achieve the intention of confidentiality. Furthermore, other control techniques, like limiting every identified user access to data system resources are utilized for maintaining confidentiality. Along with this, security against spam, malware, other attacks, spyware etc., are most significant to confidentiality.

Normally, security is the most important problem in industrial bank management and it is linked to the huge amount of bank activities. Moreover, the security of banking is ensured by computing different aspects. Apart from this, business-related bank security is a difficult structure, which includes several performances, like resource organization in the context of operational risks, market, and credit. Process security is mainly persistent on working risk and it is called the risk of failure resultant from external conditions or internal processes. Physical security is associated with the security of money in ATMs and bank branches. The security of the system involves every exterior and interior process, which is realized through an information system. The security of customer deposits is the key feature of banks and highly manipulates preservation, loss, or acquisition of customers. Therefore, it is significant for the commercial bank as the business element for undertaking various measures for ensuring suitable and effective protection of customer's deposit. Electronic banking is referred to as the body of the-information measures, which permits remote access to bank account. Electronic banking is a structure of offering banking services through electronic devices, like mobile phones, landlines, and computers. The electronic devices are utilized to accept cards, which is performed with no concurrent presence of both parties via data transfer at the request of the customer. The customers receive and transfer through devices that are particularly designed for electronic processing. Moreover, through this electronic processing method, the data are transmitted via telecommunication networks. The bank customers can perform active and passive operations and their types are dependent on the type of contract performed among customer and bank.

Normally, security is the most significant concern for every association. Many associations are troubled about the security of accumulated and transmitted data. Electronic banking and electronic commerce have their security issues, because of remote access approved to their significant information. In general, banks utilize various security methods for attaining the security needs in e-banking. Besides, various methods, such as digital signature, encryption, authentication methods, Secure Socket layer (SSL) are utilized for ensuring data transmission among bank and customer. E-banking authentication systems facing various security threats, namely fast-flux service network, pharming, spear-phishing, and whaling. In the banking industry, hardware authentications, software-based solutions, e-signatures, one- time passwords, and smart card-based solutions are introduced for providing authentication solutions. The recently developed approaches are biometrics, usage of numbers such as, Personal Identification Number, Card Verification Value, and Address Verification System to main security in the next level. AVS includes confirmation of address zip code of a customer, whereas PIN and CVM include numeric code checking, which is keyed by the customer. Similarly, biometric may include fingerprint verification and signature. Besides, geographical areas, negative and positive control register of customers, rule-based techniques are also utilized in the e-banking system.

Fraud Detection

The online banking fraud detection technique utilizes the broad-based Wisdom Web of Things (W2T) method. It also provides multi-feature data of digital banking consumers, it includes electronic fund transactions data, demographic data, credit card transactions data, and relevant types of data. These multi-aspects of data are transmitted through the Internet or World Wide Web (WWW) to the data centre. These data centre offers a platform to perform e-banking fraud recognition process. In online banking, customers, and computer systems are combined in one unit for recognizing their relationship and synchronization. In this W2T data cycle, fraud prediction is one of the most significant tasks. Many customers infrequently ensure their digital banking history recurrently and thus it is not capable of recognizing and reporting fraud transactions instantly after the occasion of fraud. This process makes the opportunity of loss revival is very less. Additionally, every alert produced from the detection system requires manual investigation and it is time-consuming. Normal, e-banking identification scheme requires very high detection rate, high accuracy, and less false positive rate. Frauds can be classified into two methods, namely offline fraud, and online fraud.

Offline fraud:

Most offline fraud events present because of a wallet or purse and it includes several important documents. The documents, like identify card, credit cards, debit cards, driving license and so on and these documents include essential information, like transaction slips, name, bank account details, and date of birth and so on.

Online fraud:

This method presents while, fraud presents their website as the real website for obtaining significant delicate data of consumer and executes legitimate transactions on particular client account.

In general cases, there are two approaches utilized to conflict the fraud, such as fraud avoidance and fraud recognition. Fraud preservation is used to sort out high-risk transactions and it is a starting process of security. Additionally, there are various authentication systems, such as expiry date, cardholder's address, signatures, and identification number are used for credit card fraud protection. Besides, the detection method is classified into two, like anomaly discovery and misuse recognition. The anomaly discovery normally used normal transactions to recognize the frauds. Likewise, misuse detection used the labelled transaction to identify the frauds. The gradually progressing cashless economy directs business movement to electronic monetary transactions and it is utilized to the accurate reorganization of fraud. Generally, fraud detection is the process of observing the transaction behaviour of the cardholder. Misuse detection types are utilized for identifying incoming transaction is fraud or not. Typically, misuse types have knowledge about present kinds of fraud for making methods through the learning of several fraud patterns. Similarly, anomaly detection type is used for creating a profile of normal transaction behaviour of cardholders using their historical transaction data. The anomaly-based fraud detection identifies whether the new transaction is different from other general transaction behaviours.

Credit card is also one of the most unauthorized kinds of fraud. A credit card is a synthetic card, which is provided to bank clients as one of the payment modes. Credit card permits the cardholders for purchasing products and goods from shopping websites or marketplace. This type of fraud involves a person uses other person's credit card for individual utilization whereas, the vendor of credit card and card issuer is not conscious about the fact that their card was used by others. The huge utilization of credit cards and deficient of efficient security methods lead to a billion-dollar loss to credit card fraud. The credit card firms are disinclined to declare information and it is complex for obtaining an accurate approximation of losses. The utilization of credit cards with a lack of tough security causes billion-dollar economic sufferers. The global economic losses that occur because of credit card fraud amount to 22.8 billion dollars in 2017 and constantly increases by 2022. In credit card fraud there are two classifications, namely behaviour fraud and application fraud. Application fraud refers to a fraud during the time of new credit card application process, by providing fake identity information and the issuer also acknowledges. Besides, behaviour fraud happens after providing credit card, accurately and it indicates credit card transactions, which includes fraud behaviour. Credit card fraud recognition is an imperative problem for financial organizations and credit card users. The fraud detection for a small amount helps to protect a huge amount of money and credit card fraud and detecting the fraudulent activities is an important issue for researches.

There are two stages, such as the Near Real-Time (NRT) stage and Real-Time (RT) Stage in the online automatic fraud detection system. The system decides rapidly whether to block a transaction using bared transaction data in the RT stage. Likewise, the system performs a slower ex-post assessment using huge information context, which involves linked data in successive NRT stage. In the NRT stage, classification rules are applied to produce awareness of doubtful transactions. Besides, doubtful transactions are transformed into human investigators for the last evaluation. Moreover, the investigator task includes selection between investigate the transaction, carrying out fast investigation on them and hence, the alert is considered as fraud transaction or legal transaction. If any transaction cases are considered fraudulent, then the consequent credit card is blocked-up. In the NRT stage, managing regulations are mainly considered. Apart from this, fraud detection in online shopping systems is a recently developing issue. The banking system, fraud investigators, and electronic payment systems, like PayPal, Gpay, etc., have an effective fraud detection system for preventing fraud performances. Using this Cyber Source information, it is needed to identify abnormalities across a prototype of fraud activities, which suffer by alternations comparative to past. The best fraud identification structure should capable to recognize fraud transactions precisely and make identification in real-time transactions. Fraud detection methods are of two types, namely misuse detection and anomaly detection. Anomaly detection system fetches trained normal transactions and it utilizes various approaches for identifying new frauds. On the other hand, misuse fraud recognition scheme utilizes labelled transaction as fraud transaction or legal transaction, which is trained by dataset history. Therefore, the misuse discovery method involves a supervised learning approach, whereas the anomaly identification structure involves an unsupervised learning method.

Globally, the credit card is one of the most significant payment methods because of the rapid growth in information technology. Credit card is in the structure of tender to obtain various products and goods however, it is one of the common methods of fraud. Generally, it is produced with stealing of real account numbers or credit cards, but still, credit fraud detection is a difficult process. Credit card fraud identification system is one of the most important concerns for various credit card users and financial organizations. Furthermore, credit card fraud arises, once a thief utilized credit card data for purchasing without the authorization of the credit card owner. The lack of security methods and large utilization of credit card normally generate billion-dollar loss in the financial network. Credit card firms are commonly disinclined to announce the information because the precise computation of financial loss estimation is a complex one. However, credit card utilization with fewer security systems generates billion-dollar economic losses in financial organizations. The huge amount of cash is gained in less time with less threat due to this reason, the credit card is considered a major source of fraud. Along with this, the credit card is produced under various kinds, such as imitation fraud, offline fraud, appliance fraud, and online fraud. The common two types of credit card fraud are termed application fraud and behaviour fraud. Application fraud occurs while, fraudulent starts a new credit card process with fake individual data thus, the issuer acknowledges the application. Likewise, behaviour fraud occurs after proper providence of credit cards and it involves fake activities during credit card transactions.

The credit card fraud is separated into two categories, namely external fraud and inner card fraud. In credit card fraud, broader classification is performed in three types, like internet fraud, merchant related frauds and traditional card related fraud. The internet fraud includes false merchant sites, credit card producers and site cloning as well as merchant related fraud involves triangulation and merchant collusion. Similarly, traditional card related fraud contains counterfeit, account takeover, stolen, fake and application. The losses due to fraud in business and banks is reached around 16 billion in 2014 and gradually increased to 2.5 billion in recent years. Normally the credit card dataset includes total transaction information. The information may contain account number, name of the account holder, merchant code, transaction date, kind of card, nature of purchase and transaction range. Some of the transaction information includes numerical type data and others in nominal types and symbolic types. Therefore, mixed data types may direct to application of extensive range of data mining techniques, machine learning and statistical approaches.

Machine Learning in Fraud Detection

In recent days, deep learning approaches are mainly considered than machine learning approaches, because of their better performance to detect fraudulent transactions. Additionally, various classification approaches are developed to detect fake credit card transactions. Normally, probabilistic neural networks, genetic programming, and logistic regression are introduced for classifying fraud in credit card transactions. Moreover, data level balanced approaches, like under-sampling approaches, easy ensemble, and oversampling approaches are efficient techniques for fraud detection. Mainly, HMM is employed for credit card fraud recognition. Alternatively, this HMM is expensive for memory and computational time. Furthermore, several approaches, like Bayesian belief network, HMM, data mining, decision tree, random forest and Artificial Neural Network (ANN) are developed for detecting fraud credit card transaction. The neural networks, namely radial basis function, feed-forward, and three-layer techniques are considered for credit card fraud transactions. The other supervised scheme using fuzzy neural network is applied for customer-specific credit card fraud transactions. Apart from this, the K-means clustering approach is commonly utilized for grouping a set of data by using similarities in elements, which is also employed for identifying credit card fraud discovery. The past transactions are labelled as legal or fake in supervised learning techniques. After that, the supervised learning techniques learning process is beings based on input data for classifying new data samples. Nevertheless, unsupervised learning techniques are developed by using direct categorization of credit card transactions based on considered patterns. Even so, both unsupervised and supervised learning approaches are utilized for detecting fraudulent credit card transactions. Generally, fraud credit card transactions are identified through categorizing the extracted features from credit card transactions. There are numerous types of classification techniques are developed for detecting fake online transactions. The Logistic Regression (LOR), Genetic Programming (GP), and Probabilistic Neural Network (PNN) are also applied to classify fraud in the online transaction. Commonly, decision trees.

Bayesian belief networks are applied for detecting fraud in financial transactions. Also, Self-Organizing Map (SOM) is widely utilized for producing unsupervised credit card fraud identification. The Long Short-Term Memory (LSTM) is employed for identifying credit card fraud in the supervised learning system, and it is sequence categorization. The deep learning techniques are also developed for supporting financial decisions.

Various machine learning approaches and statistical methods are also introduced for recognizing fraud for instance, rule-based expert system, logistic regression, decision tree and neural network. These methods are developed for detecting irregular activities and fraud detection in various domains, like credit card fraud, cash laundering, and computer interruption, etc. The fraud detection method is classified into two kinds, namely supervised and unsupervised technique. In unsupervised models, Hidden Markov Model (HMM) is normally utilized in spike detection and outlier detection, while training samples are unlabeled. Online banking can gather visibly labelled data samples based on domain knowledge and historical data. Unsupervised techniques not utilized this label information and also accuracy is lesser than supervised techniques. Various supervised techniques, like random forest and neural network are widely used in several classification applications, class imbalanced methods for fraud detection. Along with these approaches, Markov chains, neural networks, sequence alignment, and Bayesian networks are developed for fraud recognition. The credit scoring approach and data mining techniques mainly focused on statistical analysis, pattern analysis, and interpreting customer behaviour for detecting frauds.

Besides, the Discrete Wavelet Transform (DWT) is also developed for credit card fraud detection method. Commonly, a supervised machine learning technique is employed for identifying fake credit card transactions based on real-world data set. Two fraud detection methods are developed, namely the sliding window technique and ensemble approach. Moreover, bio-inspired techniques are widely utilized as a global solution for optimization issues. The bio-inspired optimization approaches are combined with machine learning methods for enhancing the performance of machine learning techniques as their capability to abstract a better solution for optimization issues. Consequently, machine learning techniques are integrated with bio-inspired optimization methods, such as the hybrid technique of auto-associative neural network model and Particle Swarm Optimization (PSO) approach to detect online fraud transactions. Hence, machine learning methods, particularly classification techniques are developed for detecting fraud transaction by neural networks, modified fisher discriminant analysis, logistic regressions, decision trees, and association rules. As raw input features are not adequate for detecting fraud transaction, feature engineering methods is developed. Moreover, domain-specific schemes are also developed for addressing verification latency and concept drift. Along with this, the ensemble method includes various representations, which show better performance than non- ensemble techniques, like Support Vector Machine (SVM), logistic regression, K Nearest Neighbour (KNN), and shallow neural network.

Improved Particle Swarm Optimization (IPSO) is a type of adaptive particle swarm optimization method for predicting fake credit card transactions. Furthermore, the KNN technique is widely utilized for identifying fraudulent credit card transactions. Normally, KNN is applied as the classification process of fraud credit card detection through estimating its adjacent point. The novel transaction is approaching and its point is close to fraud transaction, then KNN recognizes this transaction is fake. The fraud credit card detection problem is analyzed by using Chebyshev Function Link Artificial Neural Network (CFANN). This CFANN method includes two elements, such as learning and functional expansion. Also, The CFANN method is developed for identifying fraud credit cards by comparing them with decision trees and Multi-Layer Perceptron (MLP). MLP gathers the topology and it is structured into several layers. In which, the first layer is, termed as input layer, middle layer referred hidden layer. It includes more than one layer depending upon the requirements, final layer referred as output layer.

Dealing with Biomedical Data

Working with biomedical data entails working with patient data, which usually is collected in some de-identified form in a database. In such databases, there is usually missing information in the observations, both in the features, and in the labels, the latter is called censoring. Missing information in the features can in some sense be remedied by utilizing imputation, see paragraph below. We have mostly been working with registries containing patients that donate and receive hearts for transplantation. An example of such a database is the one from the United Network for Organ Sharing (UNOS), which administers the only organ procurement and transplantation network in the United States of America (UNOS, 2018). The database contains data from October 1, 1987 and onwards. In the database, there is information that encompass recipient, donor and transplant data. It includes almost 500 variables reflecting different attributes of the patients.

Major Challenges

Digital banking is widely utilized in banking sector, even though it faces various challenges as it listed below:

Password cracking It has different types of decryption approaches, but the most familiar type of method is brute force approach. It involves cracking of a person's password and username for the particular website through checking thousands of activities, words, names, and normal terms until the grouping of them is approved to the server. This cracking method does not need strong passwords; hence users frequently utilize common activities and names, which makes it easier for a password cracker to obtain access to the system.

Packet sniffers: The connection between the web server and the user's computer is sniffed for collecting a large quantity of data with regards to users as well as passwords and credit card information. The packet sniffer is used for collecting data and transfer it through network. However, it is very complex for identifying packet sniffers because, the main functionality is capturing network traffic data, not to control data stream.

Trojans: Trojan software is considered as most dangerous regarding electronic banking security because of its capability to connect in secret and transfers secret information. This program is introduced for the particular intention of communicating with no possibility of detection. Trojans are utilized for filtering data from various users, database systems, and servers. Furthermore, Trojans is installed for monitoring database communications, immediate messages, emails, and a large amount of another service.

Sever bugs: Server bugs are regularly established and patched in a sensible manner, which does not permit an attacker for utilizing threats besides an e-banking website. On the other hand, system administrations are frequently slow for implementing the latest updates, therefore an attacker permits adequate time for producing threat.

Denial of service attacks: By generating number of anonymous requests to the server, they will make the server performance drastically fall down. The server is requested for repetitively performing tasks, and it needs to utilize the vast quantity of server-side resources. The attackers will inject virus or Trojans on the user's Personal Computer and also instruct them for executing the attack on a particular server. Moreover, such attacks are employed by an opponent for interrupting the services. If the server is down, then, they have to access another server. This permits the attacker for installing malicious applications or disabling security configurations.

In the field of credit card fraud detection, neural networks have a wide range of applications. Our research study is concerned with the fundamental implementation of Neuroph. In actual, albeit restricted data was used together with a neural network with a single hidden layer to produce the findings produced. By increasing the number of transactions in the training sets and modifying the neural network design, it is possible to improve the quality of the results that are produced. Strategic relapse, choice trees, and irregular forests were among the artificial intelligence techniques used in this research to detect extortion in the charge card framework.

*****

4. Deep Learning Neural Networks

Introduction

E-commerce has come a long way since its inception. It has become an indispensable means for most companies, organizations and government agencies to increase their productivity in global trade. One of the main reasons for the success of e-commerce is the easy online credit card transaction (Lebichot2017). Whenever we talk about monetary transactions, financial fraud should also be considered. Financial fraud is a premeditated and deliberate crime in which a fraudster benefits himself by denying the victim a right or obtaining a financial gain. As credit card transactions have become a more common form of payment in recent years, fraudulent activities have increased rapidly.

We live in a fast digital world payment system. Credit card and payments companies are experiencing very rapid growth in their transaction volumes. An effective fraud detection system should be able to detect fraudulent transactions with high accuracy and efficiency. While it is necessary to prevent bad actors from executing fraudulent transactions, it is also very critical to ensure genuine users are not prevented from accessing the payments system. A large number of false positives may translate into bad customer experience and may lead customers to take their business elsewhere.

A major challenge in applying ML to fraud detection is presence of highly imbalanced data sets. In many available datasets, majority of transactions are genuine with an extremely small percentage of fraudulent ones. Designing an accurate and efficient fraud detection system that is low on false positives but detects fraudulent activity effectively is a significant challenge for researchers.

In this chapter, we apply multiple binary classification approaches - Logistic regression, Linear SVM and SVM with RBF kernel on a labeled dataset that consists of payment transactions. Our goal is to build binary classifiers which are able to separate fraud transactions from non-fraud transactions. We compare the effectiveness of these approaches in detecting fraud transactions.

Fraud Detection Process

The transactions are first checked at the terminal point to be valid or not, which is shown in Figure 4.1. At the terminal point, certain essential conditions such as sufficient balance, valid PIN (Personal Identification Number), etc. are validated and the transactions are altered accordingly. All the valid transactions are then scored by the predictive model, which then classifies the transactions as genuine or fraudulent. The investigators investigate each fraudulent alert and provide feedback to the predictive model to improve the model's performance (Pozzolo2015). This thesis only deals with the predictive model.

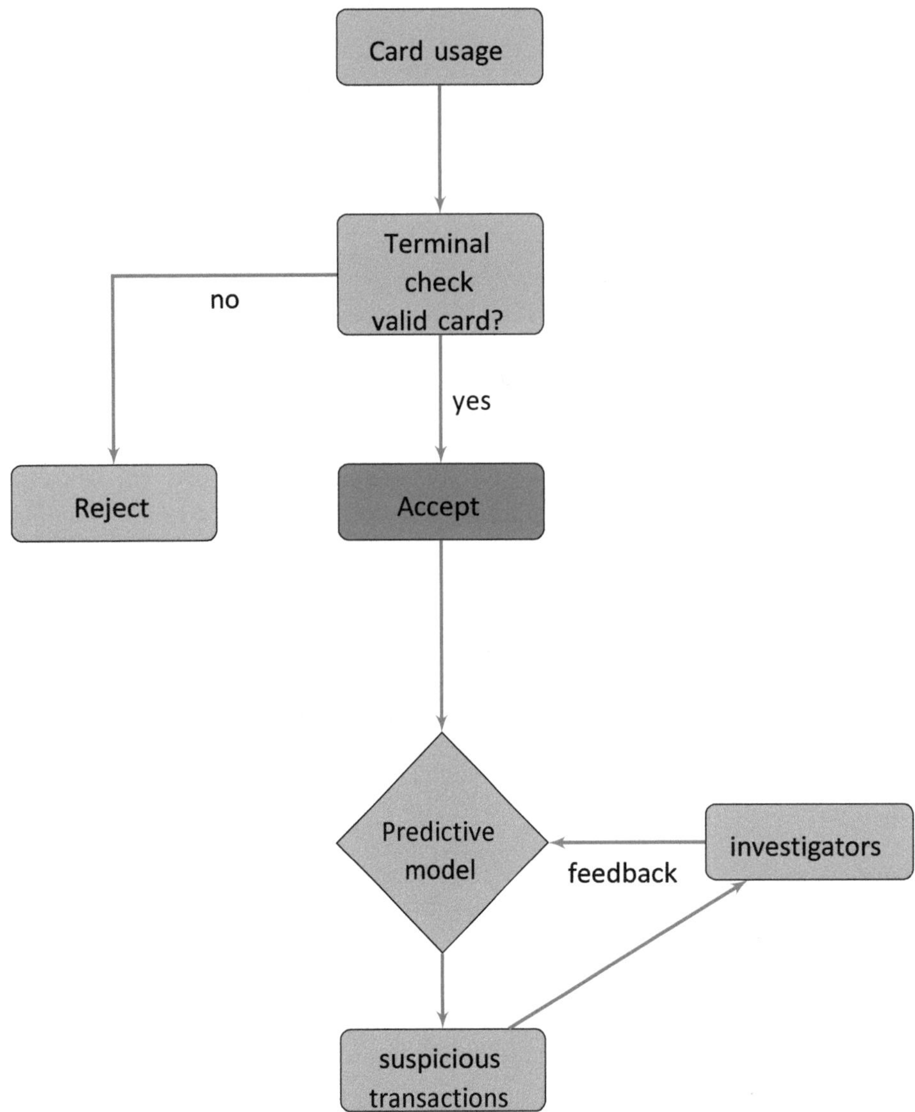

Figure 4.1: Flow chart for Fraud Detection Process

Data Description

The dataset obtained from this website: www.kaggle.com.The transactions performed by customers at a European bank over the year 2017–20 was utilized as the data set. The total number of individual transactions in the original dataset exceeds 30,000,000 in total. Each transaction record contains 62 attribute values, such as the transaction time, the transaction location, and the transaction amount. Each record is tagged with the words Fraud or Legal on it. According to the company's requirements, it is not allowed to provide specifics about the dataset's characteristics. There were about 82,000 transactions in the data set that were classified as fraudulent, resulting in a fraud ratio of 0.27 percent and a dataset imbalance issue that should be taken into account.

Methodology

With the help of this suggested system, which is both user-friendly and secure, we are now examining different fraud detection methods. It investigates the feasibility of utilizing outlier mining to identify credit card fraud, uses outlier detection mining based on distance sum to credit card fraud detection, and provides these detection methods, together with an empirical methodology, for consideration. In this article, the suggested methods are applied to the charge card framework to differentiate between extortion and fraud. Different artificial intelligence calculations, such as Logistic Regression, Decision Trees, and Random Forest, are compared to determine which one matches the data the best. These computations may be used in conjunction with charge card companies to identify extortion trades. Figure 4.2 depicts a structural diagram that covers generic gadget engineering.

The following are the stages involved in the computation of the processing steps:

Stage 1: consists of browsing through the datasets.

Stage 2: The informative index is arbitrarily checked to ensure that it has been properly calibrated.

Stage 3: Divide the dataset into two parts, one for preparation and testing purposes.

Stage 4: The suggested models are subjected to scrutiny to determine their viability.

Stage 5: The resolution was reached to determine the efficacy of various computations, including exactness and execution measures.

Stage 6: Lastly, determine which computation will provide the best results for the given dataset in Stage

Logistic Regression

Logistic regression is one of the most popular Machine Learning algorithms, which comes under the Supervised Learning technique. It is used for predicting the categorical dependent variable using a given set of independent variables. Logistic regression is a model that is used for binary classification, but it can be extended to do multiclass. The algorithm outputs a probability of the class, which can be useful. Examples of binary labels include: alive/dead, healthy/sick, or pass/fail (Medved2018). The mathematical steps to get Logistic Regression equation given below:

We know the general form of the equation of the straight line can be written as:

$$y = \beta_0 + b_1x_1 + b_2x_2 + b_3x_3 + \cdots + b_nx_n$$

Algorithm

Let t be a linear combination of the features x_i and a set of weights $w_i$wi, , where w0 is the intercept term

$$t = w_0 + w_1x_1 + \cdots + w_ix_i$$

Where w_i are the regression coefficients, indicating the relative effect of a particular feature on the outcome.

The logistic function σ, is defined and illustrated in Figure 4.2. This function is between 0 and 1 for every t. For positive infinity, it is equal to 1 and for negative it is 0. It is therefore interpretable as a probability.

$$\sigma(t) = 1/1 + e^{-t}$$

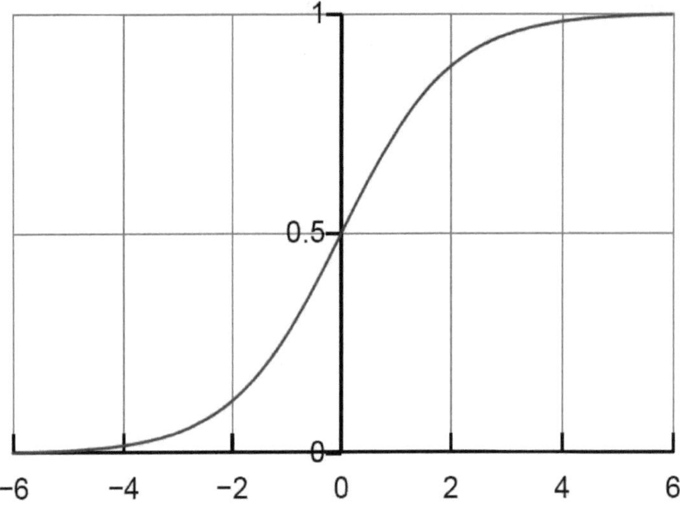

Figure 4.2: Graph of the logistic function

If we substitute t in above equation with equation, we get equation.

$$\sigma(t) = \frac{1}{1 + e^{-}\ (w_0 + w_1\ x_{1+\cdots+w_i+x_i})}$$

To go from a probability to a binary classification, we use a threshold k, which is often 0.5, see the equation.

$$\mathrm{L(t, k)} = \begin{cases} 1, & for\ \sigma(t) \geq k \\ 0, & for\ \sigma(t) \geq\ k \end{cases}$$

Fitting the model to the data means finding the weights w_i that in some senses are optimal in predicting the observations. It is possible to solve this optimization problem using several different algorithms, using for example limited-memory Broyden-Fletcher-Goldfarb-Shanno (L-BFGS) or stochastic gradient descent (SGD) (Bottou2010; Byrd1995). Often some kind of regularization is used to reduce the possible overfit, see next paragraph for more information.

Regularization

In order to minimize the possible overfit of a logistic regression model, regularization is often used. The basic idea is that an overly complex model often fits noise to the labels, thus will not generalize well to unseen data. To address this issue, a penalty term is added to the loss function, so that when we try to minimize the function, we also try to minimize the model complexity.

$$\min \sum L(y, f(x)) + \lambda R(f)$$

Where L is a loss function that describes the cost of predicting $f(x)$ when the label is y. λ controls the importance of the regularization term, *R(f)* which typically is a penalty on the complexity of f, usually a norm of model weights.

Decision Tree Algorithm

A choice tree is a controlled learning computation (i.e., one that has a pre-characterized goal variable) that is often used to deal with problems of order in mathematics. Clear-cut and consistent information, as well as yield variables, are maintained. Concerning input factors, we divide the population or test into at least two homogenous groups in light of the primary splitter/differentiator in those factors (or sub-populaces).

Decision Tree Types

Absolute Variable Decision Tree (also known as a downright factor choice tree): A downright factor choice tree is a decision tree that contains an unmitigated objective variable.

Continuous Variable Decision Tree: When the objective variable of a choice tree remains constant, the decision tree is referred to as a Continuous Variable Decision Tree.

Decision Tree Terminology

Root Node: This hub addresses the whole populace or test, which is then part into at least two homogeneous sets.

Parting: Splitting a hub into at least two sub-hubs is an activity.

Choice Node: A choice hub is framed when a sub-hub parts into more sub nodes.

Leaf/Terminal Node: A leaf or terminal hub is a hub that doesn't break.

Pruning: Pruning is the strategy for eliminating sub-hubs from a choice hub. The parting interaction can be characterized as the total inverse of parting.

Branch/Sub-Tree: A branch or sub-tree is a piece of the whole tree.

Parent and Child Nodes: A hub that is isolated into sub-hubs is alluded to as a parent hub of sub-hubs, while sub-hubs are alluded to as offspring of the parent hub.

Decision Tree in Action

Choice trees use a variety of computations to determine whether or not to divide a hub into at least two sub-hubs. With the growth of sub-hubs, the homogeneity of the following sub-hubs improves as a result. To put it another way, when the objective variable increases in value, the immaculateness of the hub becomes more apparent. Following that, the decision tree partitioning the hubs into sub-hubs based on every single available variable and then chooses the split that results in the most homogeneous sub-hubs is performed.

1. The Gini coefficient (also known as the Gini coefficient of arithmetic mean)
2. Obtaining Relevant Information
3. Square Chi is a kind of Chinese symbol.
4. Decrease in the amount of change

Artificial Neural Network

An artificial neuron consists of a linear combination of the input and its weights on the different connections. This summation is the same as in Equation 3.2. The sum is then used as input to a non-linear function known as an activation function or transfer function, see Equation 3.7. If we choose the logistic function as the activation function, see Equation 3.3, we get a function that is equivalent to logistic regression, see Equation 3.4.

$$Y = \Phi\left(\sum_{j=0}^{m} w_i \, x_i\right)$$

A neural network with the sigmoid as its activation function can therefore be seen as a network of several logistic regression models, connected in parallel and series of each other.

A network consists of three or more layers. The first layer is called the input layer, where the features are used as the initial input. The middle layers which can be one or more, are called hidden layers. Finally, the last layer, the output layer, which has as many nodes as the wanted number of outputs from the model. Figure 4.3 illustrates a network with three layers, in which the layers are fully connected.

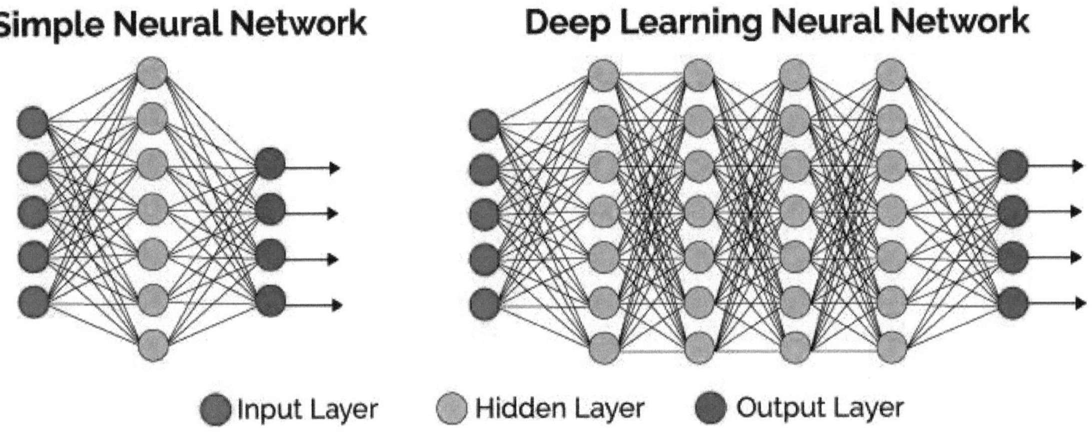

Image Source: www.thedatascientist.com

Figure 4.3: A fully connected neural network with three input nodes, four hidden nodes, and one output node.

A neural network is usually characterized by the following parameters:

- The number of hidden layers.
- The number of nodes in each layer.
- The interconnection pattern between the different layers of nodes.
- The weights of the interconnections, which are updated in the learning process.
- The activation functions, which convert a node's weighted input to its output.

A neural network using a reasonable non-linear function as its activation, such as the logistic, and one hidden layer, can be shown to approximate all continuous functions on compact subsets of Rn. An ANN is therefore in some sense a universal approximator.

Random Forest

An irregular forest calculation is a tree-based calculation that entails creating a large number of trees and connecting them to enhance the model's speculative capability. A gathering method is a tactic for bringing together a group of trees. Amassing is just the process of putting together a group of weak students (single trees) to form a strong student. Arbitrary Forest may be used to deal with a variety of problems, including relapse and disorder. When it comes to relapse problems, consistency is the most important aspect to consider. The most important variable in characterization problems is there in front of us.

The Bagging Algorithm is used to generate completely random instances. Among the informative collections are D1, which has n lines and m segments, and D2, which is a second informational index that has n cases that are randomly examined with replacement from the first information. Out of Bag tests are drawn from dataset D1, which contains 33 percent of the columns missing from the rest of the dataset. The models are then built on a second dataset, D2, and Out of Bag tests are used to determine whether or not the mistake was made fairly and objectively. M segments have browsed a sum of m segments at each hub in the informative index, resulting in a total of m segments. The main M segments are chosen at random from a pool of candidates. M is often set to m/3 for relapse trees and sqrt (m) for grouping trees, with m being the number of relapse trees. In an arbitrary forest, there is no such thing as a tree that has to be pruned; each tree is fully matured. The practice of pruning in choice trees is an effective technique for avoiding overfitting. When it comes to selecting a subtree with the lowest test failure rate, pruning is the best method. It is necessary to use cross-approval to determine the test blunder rate of a subtree. It is possible to get the final expectation by taking an average or casting a vote after many trees have been created.

Stage 1: To import the information.

Stage 2: Convert the data into information outlines.

Stage 3: Use the ROSE pack to perform arbitrary oversampling.

Stage 4: Determine how much information you'll require for preparing and exploration.

Stage 5: Give 70% of the information for preparing and the rest for research.

Stage 6: Assign the models to the preparation dataset.

Stage 7: Build the model by choosing a calculation from a rundown of three choices.

Stage 8: For every calculation, make forecasts for the test dataset.

Stage 9: Calculate exactness for every calculation.

Stage 10: For every factor, utilize a disarray network.

Stage 11: Compare the calculations for the entirety of the factors to figure out which is awesome.

The execution points were obtained via the use of the vulnerability framework. The vulnerability lattice is a network table composed of paired pairs of nodes that handle the four findings of the twofold classifier. Various measures such as affectability, exactness, accuracy, and blunder rate are calculated with the use of the disarray network algorithm. To determine exactness, divide the total number of two significant expectations (A + B) by the total number of perceptions in the dataset (C + D) and multiply the result by one hundred. It is resolved in the following manner: (an error rate of one).

$$\text{Accuracy} = \frac{A+B}{C+D}$$

Whereas,

A = True Positive; B = True Negative; C = Positive; D = Negative

Table 4.1: Accuracy Comparison Table

Algorithms	Accuracy	False Positive Rate	Recall	Precision	F1-Score
Random Forest	0.999544	0.224490	0.775510	0.950000	0.853933
Decision Tree	0.999215	0.755102	0.792857	0.773519	0.244898
Artificial Neural Network	0.999380	0.217687	0.782313	0.845588	0.812721
Naive Bayes	0.975937	0.102041	0.897959	0.060746	0.113793
Logistic Regression	0.980000	0.228687	0.742313	0.7555484	0.823832

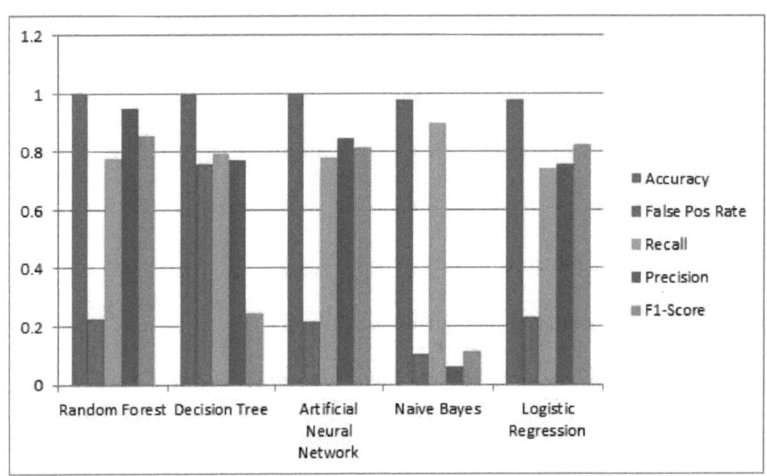

FigurE 4.4: Alogrithm Comparison

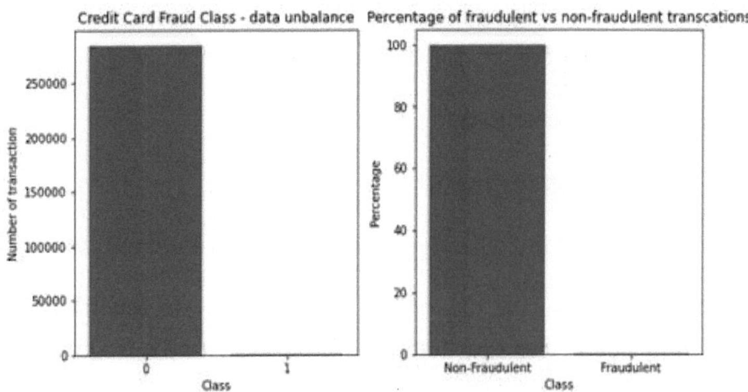

Figure 4.5: Fraud and Non Fraud Classes

Error Rate

The absolute number of two off-base forecasts (F + E) partitioned by the all-out number of the dataset (C + D) yields the blunder rate.

$$\text{Error rate} = \frac{F+E}{C+D}$$

Though,

E = False Positive

F = False Negative

C = Positive

D = Negative

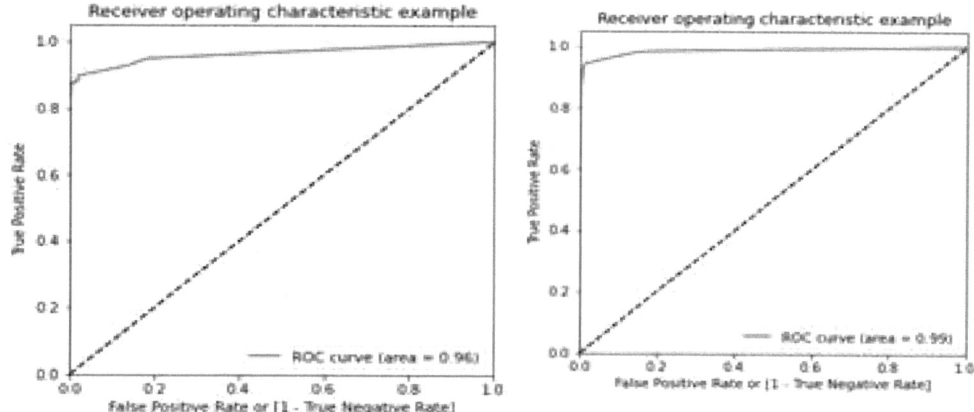

Figure 4.6: ROC Curve for Train and Test Model

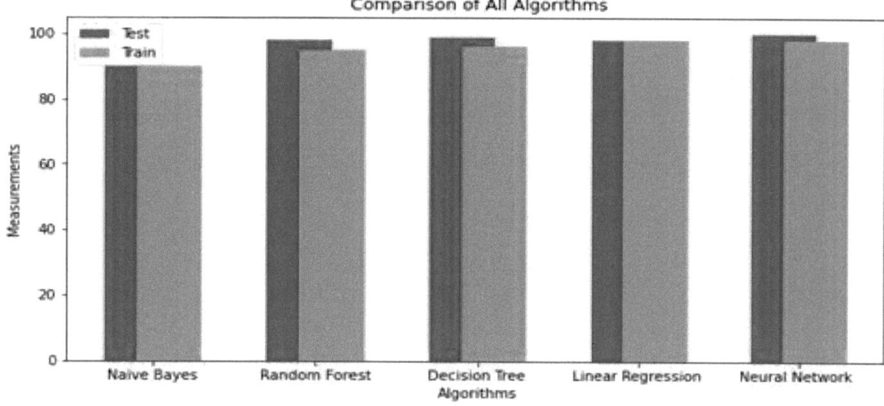

Figure 4.7: Train and Test Accuracy for All Algorithm

Affectability is controlled by separating them all outnumber of positives by the quantity of substantial positive forecasts (A) (C). The quantity of precise negative expectations (B) partitioned by the all-out number of negatives is utilized to gauge explicitness (D).

For evaluating the effectiveness of the framework in identifying charge card extortion, precision, error rate (sensitivity), and specificity (specificity) are used. Three artificial intelligence computations are implied in this article to differentiate between extortion and fraud in MasterCard settings. 70 percent of the dataset is used for arranging, and the remaining 30 percent is used for testing and evaluation to validate the computations. To demonstrate how various factors such as exactness, blunder rate, affectability, and explicitness may be used to test different factors for three calculations, Table 4.1 illustrates how they are used to test different factors for three computations. When calculating computed relapse, the exactness results for the choice tree and arbitrary timberland classifier are 92.7 percent, 95.8 percent, and 97.6 percent, respectively. As shown by the facts, the random woodlands methods outperform the calculated relapse and choice tree processes in terms of effectiveness.

Summary

The European bank transactions performed by its customers in the period 2017-2020 is considered in this chapter. The data is collected from Kaggle database. An attempt is made to detect abnormal digital transactions using Deep Learning Neural Network, Logistic Regression, Decision Tree Algorithm, Random Forest, Artificial Neural Network Algorithms are implemented in the mentioned data set of 62 attributes. The performance pf these algorithms are measured using Accuracy, False Positive Rate, Recall, Precision and F1 score. The measures are tabulated. It can be concluded that among the five algorithms. Artificial Neural Network is the better performing one to detect abnormal transactions with 99.94% 0pf accuracy.

In this chapter we have the yield of the suggested framework is evaluated by taking into account its Sensitivity, Accuracy, False rate. Using Logistic Regression, Decision Tree and Artificial Neural Network. When every one of the three methods was considered, it was discovered that the Artificial Neural Network outperformed both the calculated relapse and the choice tree techniques. It deals with an important issue of critical importance is multimodal credit card classification, and this study investigated the use of ensemble approaches to improve individual classifiers' performance in this significant work, which is of critical importance. It is surprising how effective ensemble approaches are when compared to stacking processes when the results are compared.

*****

5. Deep Learning Neural Networks Hybrid Model

Introduction

The prediction results of three classification algorithms are utilized in the suggested approach, and the final prediction is carried out using the Model Value Prediction method, which is described below. The categorization of credit-cards is implemented in this study via the use of Python scripting. In addition, python packages such as NumPy, scipy, scikit-learn, TensorFlow, and Keras are utilized in the development of this suggested system, as well as other programming languages. Figure 2 shows implantation steps draw to the proposed scheme.

Data Set

The datasets used in this investigation were obtained from the Kaggle competition. The Kaggle dataset contains 31 attributes, 28 of which are anonymized and classified as V1-V28 in the V1-V28 classification system. The final three parameters are the time of the transaction, the amount, and the label of fraud. Anonymization has been applied to the variables (because these are genuine European cardholder transactions). There are 284,807 transactions in total in this dataset. It is possible to spend anywhere from 88.35 USD to 25,691.16 USD on a single transaction. As predicted, the majority of transactions are modest in nature. The amount of time that has elapsed since the first transaction in the dataset is measured in seconds. The transactions take place over the course of two days. In this sample, only 0.17 percent of transactions were fraudulent, according to the data. Additionally, there is little association between factors. It is possible that this is due to CNN transformed variables. As a result, my mode does not have to account for multi co linearity.

Table 5.1: Split Dataset

Datass	Training	Testing	Total
Fraud	44	15	59
Non-Fraud	46	15	61
	90	30	120

Data augmentation is carried out on the training dataset after pre-processing. The result of the data augmentation process will increase the training dataset size to 360 shown in table 5.1.

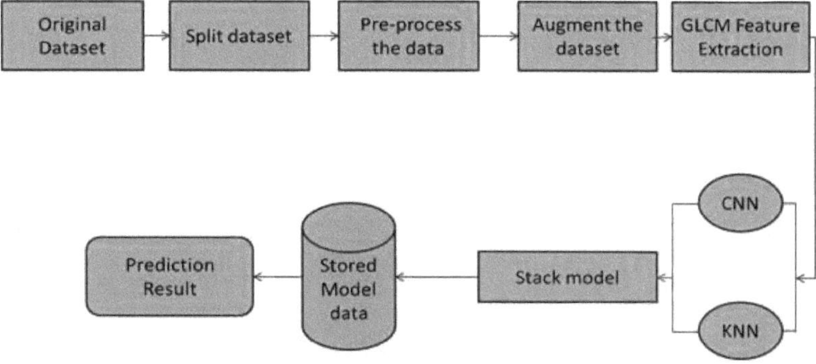

Figure 5.1: Proposed Architecture

The architecture of the Proposed Model

To begin, import the original MR datass into the computer for pre-processing. Following that, individually do thresholding on the MR datass to transform them into binary datass. In addition, privately conduct the dilation and erosion procedures to eliminate noise from the datass captured. After that, computed the four extreme points (extreme top, extreme bottom, extreme right, and extreme left) of the threshold datass by selecting the contour with the greatest area of the threshold datass and selecting the largest contour of the threshold datass. Finally, crop the datas based on the information provided by the contour and extreme point information. Figure() shows bicubic interpolation is used to enlarge the credit-card datass that have been clipped. This method is preferred over other interpolation methods such as bilinear interpolation because it produces a smoother curve than other methods such as bilinear interpolation.

Data Pre-Processing and Augmentation

The fact that I don't have a lot of information about the exact timing of the transaction has led me not to include it in the first assessment of its impact. I could hypothesize that the majority of the fraudulent activity occurs at night, but I have opted to exclude this variable from the first study. I have also standardized the quantity variable (Standard Deviation) because of the large volatility in the quantity variable. Because the number of observations in my project is not expected to be large, the split distribution for Train-Development-Test is 60-20-20 in favor of the former. Additionally, I utilized a 5 split stratified sampling approach known as sss1 = Stratified Shuffle Split (n splits = 5, test size = 0.2, random state = 42) together data (n splits = 5, test size = 0.2, random state = 42). As a result of the restricted quantity of fictitious data available, I utilized an oversampling strategy: ADASYN (sampling strategy='minority, random state=42) to get the desired results. Both negative and positive correlations were found in the balanced sample, indicating that both are present. In the case of the traits V14, V12, V10, and V3, there is a negative relationship between them and the word "Class." The balanced training data (which has been oversampled) is divided into 700 batches and 40 epochs. There were three baseline models employed: Logistic Regression, Random Forest, and GaussianNB, all of which had been previously built and verified before being deployed. After that, I used a multilayer perception (with both 1 and 2 hidden layers), which also had both 1 and 2 hidden layers, for the next 100 iterations, and so on. There were 65 neurons in the first dense layer. Drop out was also used to reduce the deviation between the train and the val. The F-score was employed as a criterion for assessing performance. I've also trained GAN to improve the fraudulent dataset by reducing cross-entropy loss, which is a loss of information (defined as a measure of how accurately the discriminator identified real and generated datass). The modified dataset was sent through a first conv layer (32 filters with width 5) before being fed via a fully connected dense layer (64 neurons) and, finally, through a softmax prediction method to arrive at the final result. Because there is no spatial organization among the variables in the credit card dataset, I transformed the convolution networks to networks with densely linked layers to better represent the data. The three deep learning models that I have used in this research are a two-layer MLP, a GAN, and two 1-D Conv layers (kernel size 29), max pooling, and a fully connected dense layer (tested with 65 and 300 neurons) that terminates with a softmax function (see the following figure) (2 class prediction). With the ADAM optimization and the loss function for GAN, a total of 2000 epochs were run with the resultant data.

Table 5.2: Augmentation Data split-up

Datass	Training	Testing	Total
Fraud	140	50	190
Non-Fraud	120	50	170
	260	100	360

Feature Extraction

This procedure reduces the size of the dataset to more manageable characteristics for processing, while still properly and completely representing the original dataset. It is used in data mining and machine learning applications. Informational and non-redundant, it is meant to facilitate the subsequent learning and generalization phases, which in certain situations will result in superior human interpretations. When dealing with large amounts of data, there are several alternative feature selection models to consider.

Table 5.3: Feature Extraction Parameter Values

Mean	Standard Deviation	Skewness	Kurtosis	Energy	Entropy
39	61	0.00553	2.890	10.94	0.65
117	210	0.00655	2.740	16.37	0.94
39.40	75.59	0.01054	1.850	65.99	3.03
6.83	39.45	0.00517	3.333	8.11	0.45
11.90	38.81	0.02002	1.354	33.17	2.09
5.33	28.95	0.01647	2.054	13.87	1.12

Methods and Classification

Stack Ensemble

This is a strategy for integrating numerous classification or regression models into a single model that is known as stacking. Model construction may be accomplished via a number of approaches. Stacking is required in order to study the space of various models for the same problem. You may approach a learning problem using a variety of different models, each of which can only learn a fraction of the problem space and is hence ineffective when applied over a large amount of problem space. A byproduct of this is that you may generate many different learner models, which you can then use to produce an intermediate prediction, one prediction for each learnt model that you have built. Then you add a new model that learns from the intermediate predictions and learns to achieve the same objective as the prior model, and you repeat the procedure. As a result of the way this final model is built on top of the others, it is referred to as a "stacked model." Consequently, you may see an increase in your overall performance, and you may even end up with a model that is better than any single intermediate model as a consequence. However, it should be noted that, as is generally the case with any machine learning technology, it does not give any assurances. Model stacking is an ensemble approach that is used to merge a varied number of classification algorithms into a single classification system. Model stacking is a technique that allows many model predictions to be combined in order to attain higher predictive performance. Some of the categorization techniques that are used are assemblies in and of themselves. K-NN classifiers are used for bagging assemblies, while CNN classifiers are used for ensemble boosting. CNN classifiers can improve their accuracy and minimize overfitting by training a large number of decision-making bodies at the same time and then merging their predictions. By raising the gradient, K-NN classifiers, on the other hand, may reduce distortion while simultaneously enhancing accuracy.

Methodology

1. Subdivide the training dataset into n pieces of equal size and length.
2. A basic model (for example, linear regression) is fitted on n-1 components, and predictions for the nth component are generated based on the results of the fit. This operation is performed for each of the n parts that make up the train set in question.
3. The last phase involves fitting the base model to the whole train dataset, which is the final step.
4. The outcomes of the test dataset will be predicted using the model that was developed.
5. The exact same steps are performed again using a different base model to provide a whole new set of predictions for both training and testing data sets.
6. In order to construct the new model, the predictions made on the train data set are used as a feature in the development process.
7. The predictions that were generated on the test dataset were based on the final model that was created.

Parameters	Test Accuracy %	Sensitivity %	Specificity %
Stack Ensemble Algorithm	98.33	97.5	76.54

K-Nearest Neighbour

When it comes to classification techniques, K-NN is a simplistic approach that works well in real-time applications. This example has class labels as well as a collection of tuples that are connected to those labels, which makes the training process simple and uncomplicated. This strategy is successful for modules with a random number of components since the elements are distributed evenly. When mapping samples to classes, the K-NN classification model makes use of the distance function to determine which samples belong to which classes. When calculating the distance between the supposed test illustration X and the existing examples y1, y2, and yk, it is required to use the K-NN classification algorithm, which can be found here. They are chosen by identifying which neighbours are the closest to the test instance, and the majority of neighbourhood lectures are given to the test samples based on the selection of neighbours made during the selection process. Depending on the circumstance, the distance function is applied between the samples using the Euclidean technique, the Manhattan method, or the Minkowski method, with the distance function being applied between the samples using the Euclidean approach. When the values are continuous, various strategies are used in order to get the desired outcomes. It is reliant on the number of neighbours that each sample receives as a result of the sample X probability assigning each sample. In the case of sample X being allocated to a class C, the probability of assigning the sample to that class is proportional to the number of neighbours considered, which is denoted by the letter K. The accuracy of the K-NN classifier is shown in Table 5.4.

Makowski Function: $(\sum k_i |x_i - y_i|)1/q$

Table 5.4: Accuracy Table for K-NN Classifier

Parameters	Test Accuracy %	Sensitivity %	Specificity %
K-NN Algorithm	88.33	92.3	78.5

Convolution Neural Networks

Convolution neural networks are a sort of deep neural learning network that may be used to evaluate and classify datas in a variety of applications. The attributes of the input datas are extracted by a CNN during operation. The datas passes through a number of layers before reaching the final fully connected layer, which classifies the data's based on "voting." This layer is often composed of convolutions, ReLU, and pooling layers. The accuracy of the CNN classifier is shown in Table 5.5.

$$O_s = b_s + \sum W_{st} . X_t$$

Table 5.5: Accuracy Table for CNN Classifier

Parameters	Training Accuracy %	Sensitivity %	Specificity %
CNN Algorithm	84.3	96.48	87.3

Results and Discussion

When used in conjunction with stack ensemble perception, the proposed method performs preprocessing feature extraction and classification in the same way that stack ensemble perception does. This identifies various objects, different textures, contrast, brightness, and depth of the data in the same way that stack ensemble perception does. More to the point, if certain medications are effectively employed, the applicability of the proposed strategy may be broadened to embrace a greater range of cancers as well as MR modalities other than those now accessible. Individuals wish to investigate how well the recommended technique works in more realistic and clinically limited settings, using a dataset that has a diverse range of scenarios with a variety of various attributes. Table 5.6 displays the area of the recovered credit-card, as well as a comparison with the area assessed by expert radiologists, respectively.

Table 5.6: Accuracy of classification based on feature extraction is measured

Classifiers	Accuracy (%) without features extraction	Accuracy (%) with features extraction
K-NN	84.25	88
CNN	89.53	97.50
Stacked	90.54	98.33

Table 5.7: A comparison of the accuracy of various classifiers is shown

Parameters	K-NN	CNN	Stack Ensemble
False Positive	53	60	59
False Negative	53	57	59
Specificity (%)	78.5	87.3	76.54
Sensitivity (%)	92.3	96.48	97.5
Accuracy (%)	88.33	97.50	98.33

Following the numerous assessment criteria, Table 5.7 provide an overview of the categorization analysis of the results of each of the suggested models, which is organized in accordance with the various evaluation criteria. As seen in the table, the K-NN model has the lowest specificity (78.5 percent) and the highest sensitivity (100 percent), making it the best choice (92.3 percent). It also outperformed the CNN model in terms of sensitivity (97.48 percent), specificity (76.54 percent), and accuracy (987.50 percent), all of which were higher than the K-NN model. With a sample size of just 96.47 percent, the Ensemble Model achieved an acceptable classification result, as measured by the sensitivity of 96.4 percent, the specificity of 87.3 percent, and the accuracy of 98.0 percent, among other parameters. For its part, the Ensemble Model has shown superior performance, demonstrating the highest levels of sensitivity, specificity, and accuracy among the available models.

$$\text{Test Accuracy K-NN} = \frac{\text{(False Positive+False Negative)}}{\text{(Total Test Dataset)}} \times 100 = 106\ 120 \times 100 = 88.3$$

$$\text{Test Accuracy Stacked Ensemble} = \frac{\text{(False Positive+False Negative)}}{\text{(Total Test Dataset)}} \times 100 = 118\ 120 \times 100 = 98.33.$$

$$\text{Test Accuracy CNN} = \frac{\text{(False Positive + False Negative)}}{\text{(Total Test Dataset)}} \times 100 = 117\ 120 \times 100 = 97.50.$$

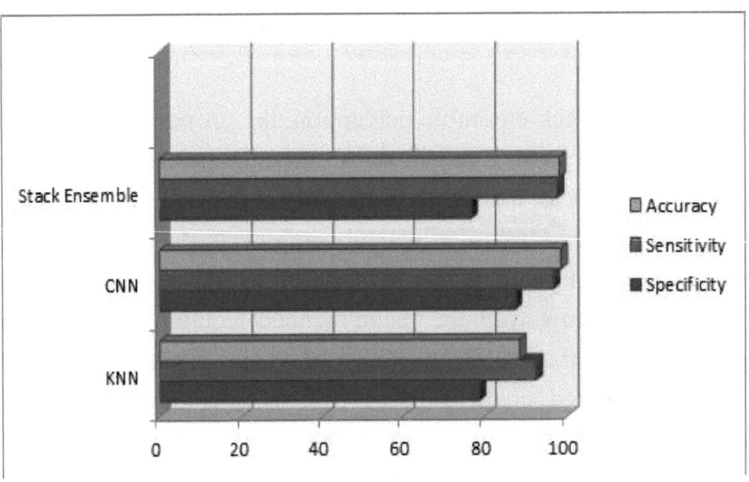

Figure 5.2: Accuracy-performance

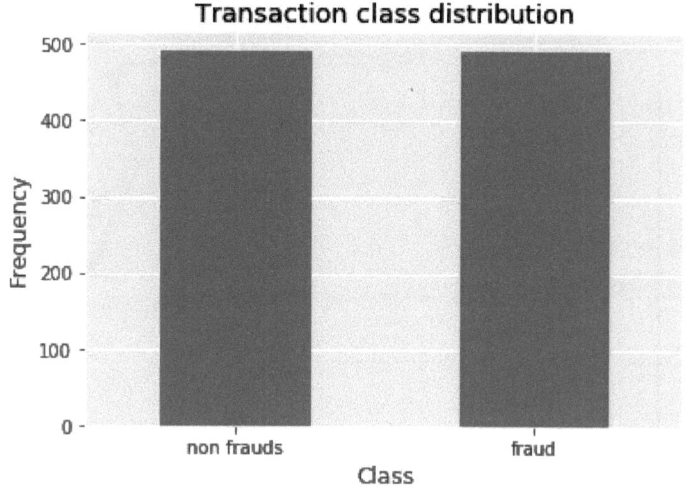

Figure 5.3: Transaction Class Distribution

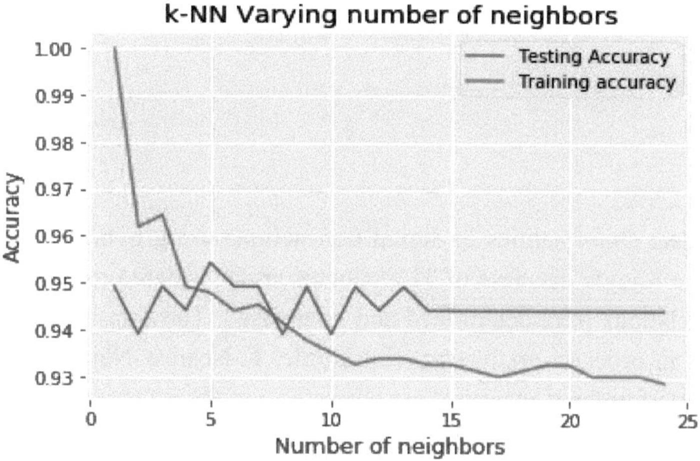

Figure 5.4: KNN Test and Train Accuracy

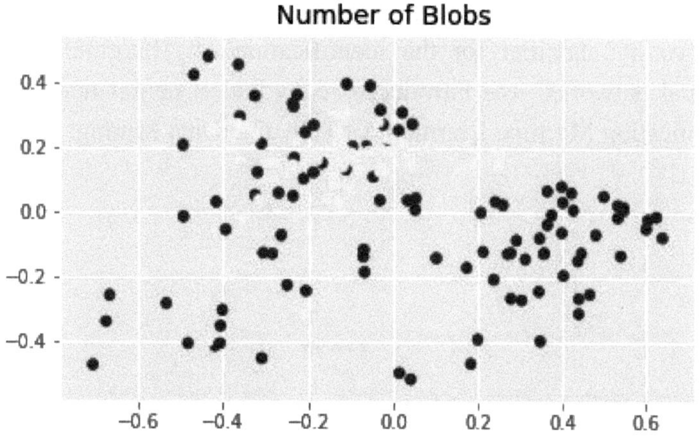

Figure 5.5: Number of Blob

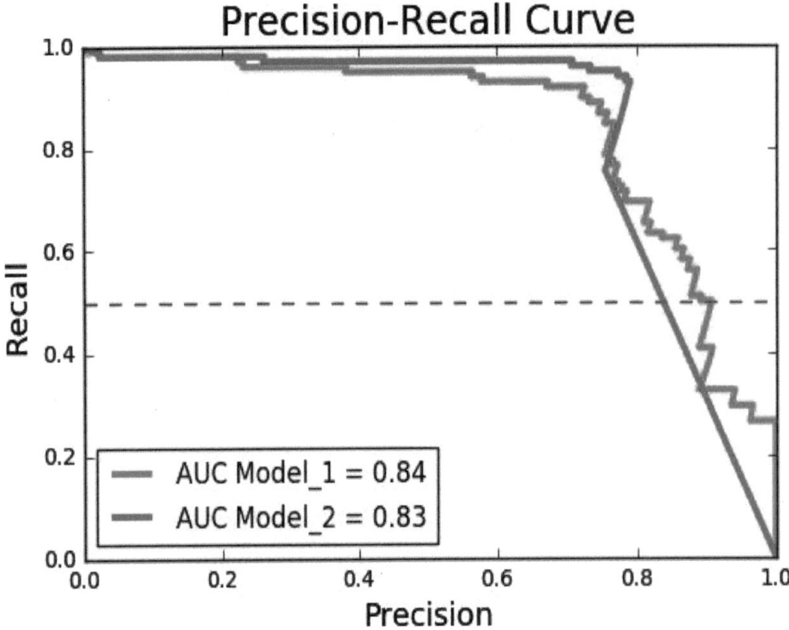

Figure 5.6: Precision and Recall Curve

Summary

This chapter attempt to detect abnormalities in digital transactions using hybrid deep learning neural networks. The data set, taken from the Kaggle database of 31 attributes are considered to implement the algorithms. In the preprocessing step the correlations were determined and interpreted. The data is splitted up in augmentation step. The features are extracted in order to apply stack Ensemble, K-Nearest Neighbors and Convolutional Neural Networks Algorithms. The performance measures are tabulated and the accuracy of K-NN, CNN, Stack Ensemble methods are 88.33%, 97.50% and 98.33% respectively. It is found that the stack Ensemble algorithm is performing better in the data set in detection of abnormal transactions.

Specifically, whether ensemble approaches may increase the classification accuracy of individual classifiers in the context of k-Nearest Neighbours is the first topic to be addressed. According to the data reported in this paper as an ensemble majority voting classifier for the identification of Abnormal transactions, an entirely new approach, convolution neural networks, was introduced: convolution neural networks for transaction data and abnormal transaction identification Machine Learning for Effective Data Mining: Algorithms and Approaches 76 (CNNs).

*****

6. Credit Card Fraud Detection using Artificial Neural Networks

Introduction

When someone uses another person's credit card without that person's permission, credit card fraud occurs. This can happen with or without the physical card when the necessary information, such as the PIN, password, and other credentials, are stolen. We can determine whether or not the upcoming transaction is fraudulent using a fraud detection module that uses machine learning and deep learning. Nowadays, the majority of them use credit cards to buy items they desperately need but cannot currently afford. Credit cards are used to fulfill the needs, and the fraud that goes along with it is growing. A model that fits well and predicts with greater accuracy must be developed and put into use as a result.

Machine learning is the most prevalent and widely utilized technology because of its many uses, quick turnaround times, and reliable outcomes. Machine learning is a field of technology that deals with the algorithms that give computers the ability to learn from experience and develop without being explicitly programmed. The use of machine learning is widespread. Combining algorithms and statistical models in machine learning enables computers to carry out tasks without the need for hard coding. A model is built using training data, and it is then tested using the trained model.

Types of Credit Card Frauds

On e-commerce websites, frauds of all stripes can be seen. In a number of methods, including those used by Fu2016, Ghosh1994, Sahin2011 and nielsen2015neural the researchers were taught with actual data by banks. While online theft can happen via the internet and mobile phones, offline theft and robberies happen close to ATMs.

Application fraud: The fraudster steals the customer's login information before creating a phoney account and doing the transactions.

Manual or electronic card imprints: The fraudster will read the card's information, utilize the credentials, and conduct the fraudulent transaction.

Card not present: This is a transaction where the actual physical card is not present.

Fraud involving counterfeit cards: The fraudster copies all of the magnetic strip data from cards that seem identical to the real thing in order to commit fraud.

Lost or stolen card: This can happen if the cardholder loses it or if someone steals it from them. Card id theft: This happens when the id of the cardholder stolen and fraud takes place.

Letter non-received card fraud: When a credit card issued, a mail will send to the recipient. Fraud here might happen through mail fraud or phishing.

Account Takeover: In this method, the fraudster seizes total authority over the account holder in order to commit fraud.

Website fake fraud: The fraudster will insert harmful code that performs their actions in the website.

Merchant collision: Without the cardholder's consent, the merchants share the cardholder's information with a third party or a fraudster.

Credit card use has become a more common method of payment because to advancements in e-commerce and communication technology, and transaction fraud is also on the rise, according to Taha2020. They employed the optimized light gradient boosting machine, which combines Bayesian-based hyper-parameter optimization with light gradient boosting machine parameter tuning (LightGBM). They employed two sets of real worlds, publicly available datasets, including both fraudulent and non-fraudulent transactions, in this method. Their proposed approach outperformed other techniques in terms of accuracy when compared. Accuracy is 98.40%, area under the receiver operating characteristics curve (AUC) is 92.88%, precision is 97.34%, and the F1-score is 56.95% for the proposed system.

According to studies by Makki2019, credit card theft results in significant financial losses. The majority of researchers have been working on this to offer a cutting-edge technique to eliminate this loss, but the majority of the approaches that are currently available are expensive, time-consuming, and labor-incentive tasks. After conducting numerous experimental experiments, the authors concluded that the uneven used the balanced dataset in order to train these models.

Several authors, including Jiang2018 have proposed a novel, multi-stage process. The process begins with the collection of cardholder transactions, followed by the aggregated transactions based on behavioural patterns, classification of the dataset, training of the model, and testing of the model. In the event that any anomalous behaviour occurs, the system is given input via a feedback mechanism.

The ratio of credit card fraud to regular transactions is a little bit appropriate, thus Ishan Sohony, Rameshwar Pratap, and Ullas Nambiar presented an ensemble learning strategy. They discovered that neural networks and Random Forest work best together to deliver a higher level of accuracy for identifying fraud incidents. They also conducted experiments using significant real-world credit card transactions. Neural networks and Random Forest are combined in ensemble learning.

According to study by Phuong Hanh Tran, Kim Phuc Tran, Truong Thu Huong, Cédric Heuchenne, Phuong Hien Tran, and Thi Minh Huong Le, credit card fraud has gradually increased over the past few years. Machine-learning algorithms are used in a variety of ways to find and stop fraudulent transactions. Two novel data-driven methodologies were introduced, using the best anomaly strategy for credit card transaction fraud. The two methods are the T2 control chart and choosing the kernel parameters.

According to Imane Sadgali, Nawal Sael, and Faouzia Benabbou's research, people today prefer digital and paperless transactions, hence financial transactions like internet, credit card, and mobile ones are becoming more and more common. Millions of transactions were made, and every single one of them was the victim of fraud. Numerous academics have examined, created, and developed the concept for applying machine learning to detect fraud. To determine which model is optimal for fraud detection in card transactions, they presented a comparison of the completely machine-learning methodology. To assess the precision of fraud detection, Debachudamani Prusti and Santhnu Kumar Rath created an application using machine learning techniques such as Decision Tree (DT), K-Nearest Algorithm (KNN), Extreme Learning Machine (ELM), Multilayer Perceptron (MLP), and Support Vector Machine (SVM). Through the fusion of the DT, SVM, and KNN approaches, they created a model. For effective data interchange across numerous heterogeneous systems, they employed two web-based protocols called Simple Object Access Protocol (SOAP) and Representational State Transfer (REST). Based on an accuracy parameter, the results of five machine-learning algorithms were compared. SVM outperformed other algorithms by 81.63 percent, while their proposed hybrid system had a higher accuracy rate of 82.58%. Unsupervised credit card fraud detection method employing autoencoder-based clustering was proposed by Mohamad Zamini and Golamali Montazar. When evaluated on a European dataset and compared to other systems, they performed well using three hidden layers and k means for clustering.

The artificial neural network is used by the proposed method to detect fraud in credit card transactions. Based on prediction, performance is evaluated and accuracy is calculated. The dataset used in the experiment consist of 12 and so on and last attribute give the outcome of the transaction in either 0 or 1.

Methodology

Scatter plots display the relationship between two continuous variables by placing one variable on the x-axis and another on the y-axis. The input variable is on the x-axis of a scatter plot for regression, while the response variable is on the y-axis. You may generally assess if there is a linear link between several variables by using scatter plot matrices. This is especially useful for identifying particular characteristics that might correlate with the credit card datasets.

According to Ciaburro2017, ANN is a term used to describe a collection of nonlinear statistical modelling techniques that are based on and inspired by the structure of the human brain. ANNs are particularly adapted to the problem of detecting credit card fraud since they may be used to simulate any complex transactional pattern. A neuron is the fundamental building block of a neural network. It accepts several inputs, adds them up, applies a transfer function (often nonlinear), and then generates the result as either a model prediction or as input to other neurons. A neural network is a structure made up of numerous such neurons that are systematically connected. Feed-forward neural networks, commonly referred to as multilayer perceptrons, are the most widely used neural networks.

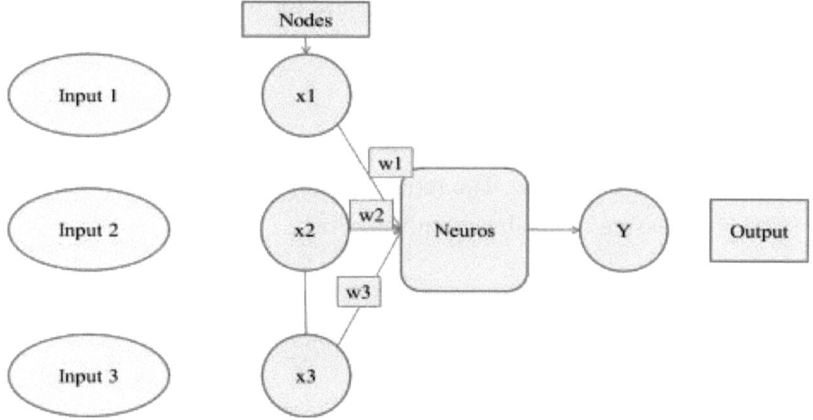

Figure 6.1: Architecture of Artificial Neural Network

The biological model for ANN is the human brain. In the human brain, neurons are connected in the same way as nodes are connected in an artificial neural network. The construction of an ANN with input, output, and hidden layers is shown in Figure 6.1. The inputs are $x_1, x_2, \ldots, x_n$ and the output is y. The weights for each of the inputs, $w_1 \ldots w_n$. This neural network employs three hidden layers.

Confusion Matrix

A confusion matrix is a table that is used to describe how well a classification system performs. A confusion matrix depicts and summaries a classification algorithm's performance. Four fundamental properties (numbers) are comprised of the confusion matrix and used to specify the classifier's measuring metrics. These four numbers are:

TP (True Positive): TP represents the number of frauds who have properly classified to have malignant nodes, meaning they have the fraud.

TN (True Negative): TN represents the number of correctly classified credit card users who are non-fraud.

FP (False Positive): FP represents the number of misclassified customers with the fraud but actually, they are non-fraud. FP is also known as a Type I error.

FN (False Negative): FN represents the number of customers misclassified as non-fraud but actually, they are fraud. FN known as Type II error.

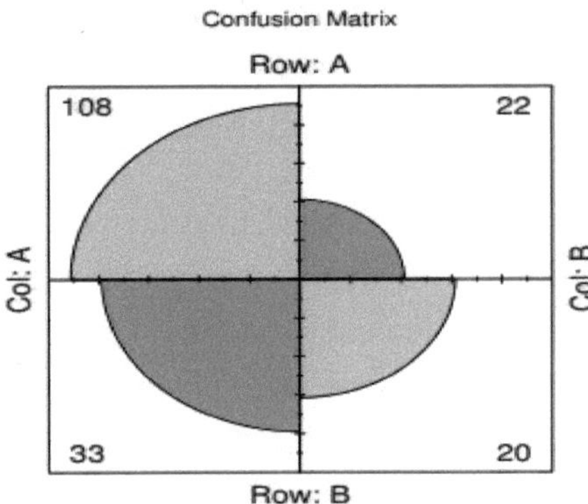

Figure 6.5: Confusion Matrix

Figure 6.5, represent the confusion matrix for predicted class for fraud and non-fraud. The left upper and right lower values are the correctly predicted and others are wrongly classified that means true positive, true negative, false positive and false negative.

Accuracy, precision, recall, and F1 score are performance metrics for algorithms that are determined using the TP, TN, FP, and FN shown in figure 6.2 below. The ratio of patients who were correctly classified (TP+TN) to all patients (TP+TN+FP+FN) is a measure of an algorithm's accuracy.

	Actually Positive (1)	Actually Negative (0)
Predicted Positive (1)	**True Positives (TPs)**	**False Positives (FPs)**
Predicted Negative (0)	**False Negatives (FNs)**	**True Negatives (TNs)**

Figure 6.2: Confusion Matrix Plot

Output of the Analysis

Model the data split in terms of training and testing data 80/20 before executing the artificial neural network. The correlation between the variables and scatter plot explained in Figure 6.3 along with a full histogram. In contrast to the other variables, the correlation between the two variables for housing and credit history is extremely positive. When compared to other variables, the Foreign Workers (V20) and Other Debtors (V12) have a very low correlation.

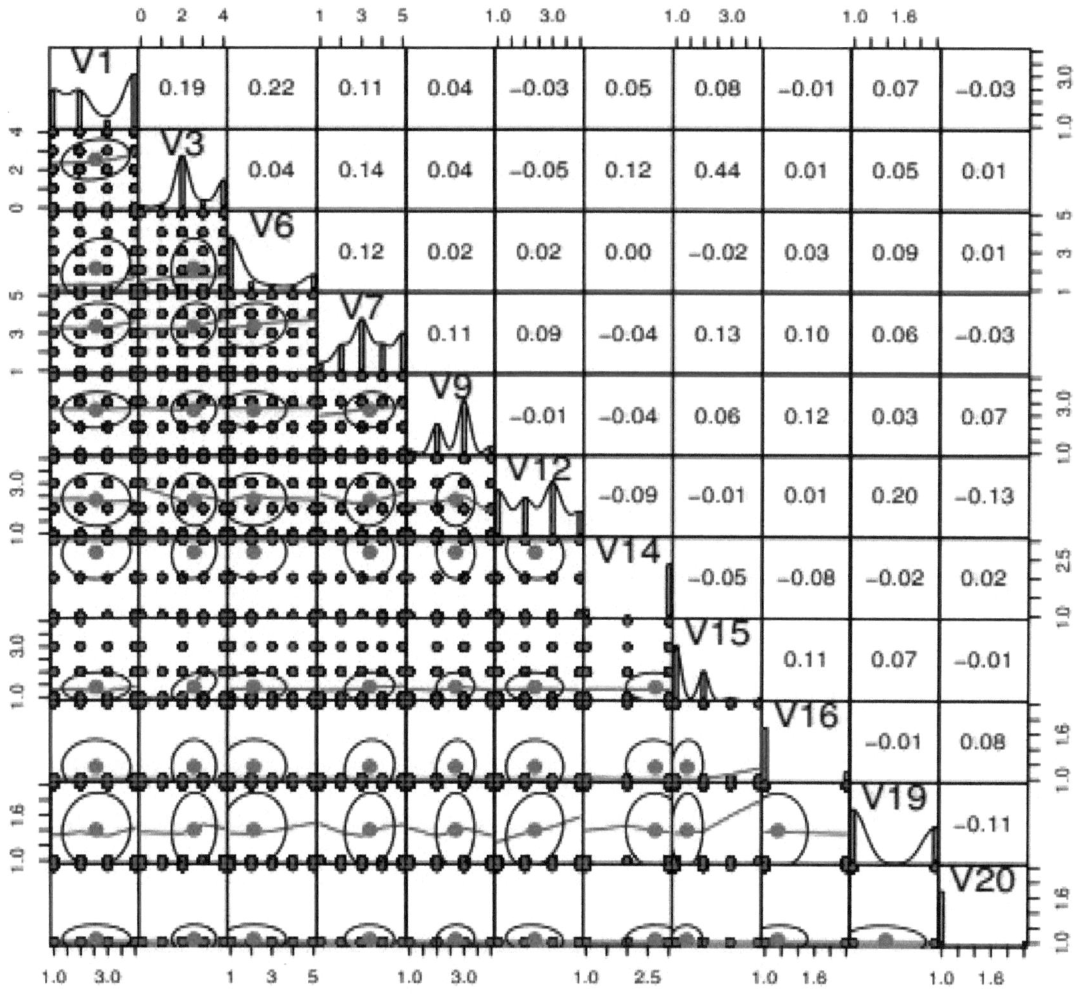

Figure 6.3: Scatter plot Matrix

Artificial Neural Network

The Figure 6.4 represent the left-most nodes (i.e., input nodes) are the raw data variables for German Credit Card data. The arrows in black (and associated numbers) are the weights which say that how much that variable contributes to the next node. The blue lines are the bias weights. The middle nodes (i.e., anything between the input and output nodes) are the hidden nodes. This is where the image analogy helps. Each of these nodes constitutes a component that the network is learning to recognize.

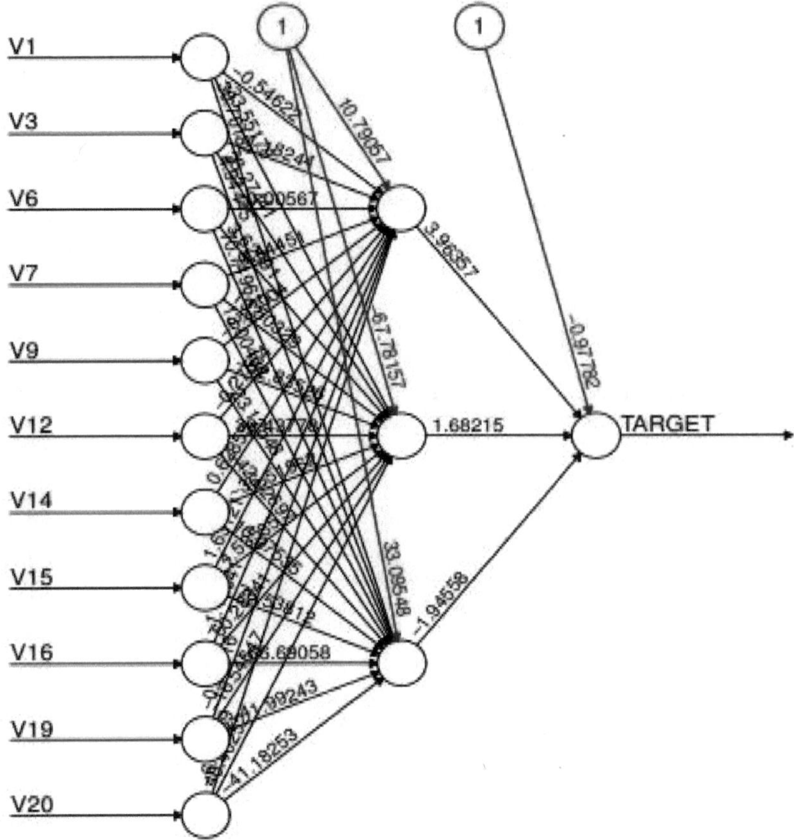

Figure 6.4: Artificial Neural Network for Credit Card Fraud

Overall Statistics

Table 6.1 represent the overall measures for the collected dataset. The ANN model overall model accuracy is 70% and Sensitivity and Prevalence are 0.77. The balance accuracy is 0.63. In machine learning methods more than 70 percentage of accuracy is the acceptable fit. Furthermore, the Artificial Neural Network model was well fitted with the help of three hidden layers and prediction also fitted.

Table 6.1: overall Statistics

Accuracy	0.70
Kappa	0.22
Sensitivity	0.77
Specificity	0.48
Prevalence	0.77
Balance Accuracy	0.63
Mcnemar's Test P value	0.18

```
Model: "sequential"
_________________________________________________________________
Layer (type)                 Output Shape              Param #
=================================================================
dense (Dense)                (None, 6)                 186
_________________________________________________________________
dense_1 (Dense)              (None, 20)                140
_________________________________________________________________
dense_2 (Dense)              (None, 10)                210
_________________________________________________________________
dense_3 (Dense)              (None, 1)                 11
=================================================================
Total params: 547
Trainable params: 547
Non-trainable params: 0
_________________________________________________________________
```

Figure 6.6: ANN Model

```
Epoch 1/10
1994/1994 [==============================] - 3s 1ms/step - loss: 0.1319 - accuracy
: 0.9983
Epoch 2/10
1994/1994 [==============================] - 2s 1ms/step - loss: 0.0047 - accuracy
: 0.9982
Epoch 3/10
1994/1994 [==============================] - 2s 985us/step - loss: 0.0029 - accura
cy: 0.9995
Epoch 4/10
1994/1994 [==============================] - 2s 955us/step - loss: 0.0028 - accura
cy: 0.9994
Epoch 5/10
1994/1994 [==============================] - 2s 969us/step - loss: 0.0032 - accura
cy: 0.9993
Epoch 6/10
1994/1994 [==============================] - 2s 999us/step - loss: 0.0027 - accura
cy: 0.9994
Epoch 7/10
1994/1994 [==============================] - 2s 1ms/step - loss: 0.0026 - accuracy
: 0.9995
Epoch 8/10
1994/1994 [==============================] - 2s 1ms/step - loss: 0.0028 - accuracy
: 0.9994
Epoch 9/10
1994/1994 [==============================] - 2s 1ms/step - loss: 0.0024 - accuracy
: 0.9995
Epoch 10/10
1994/1994 [==============================] - 2s 1ms/step - loss: 0.0026 - accuracy: 0.9995
```

Figure 6.7: ANN EPOCHS

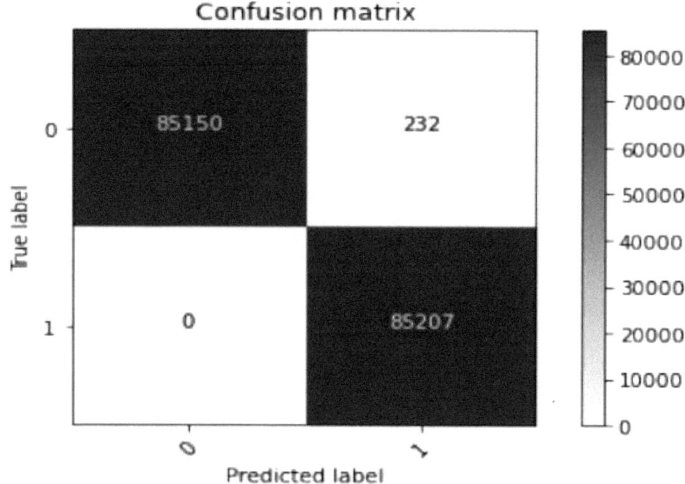

Figure 6.8: Confusion Matrix

Summary

This chapter attempts to detect credit card fraud using neural networks. Artificial Neural Network, a widely used neural network is implemented. German credit card dataset is considered to develop the model and the dataset consists of 12 features. The data is depicted by scatter plot matrices. The correlation measures are determined and it is found that the relationship between housing and credit history is high; on the other hand, the relationship between foreign workers and other debtors is extremely low. Then the Artificial Neural Network is constructed with three hidden layers and the predicted classes are mentioned using the confusion matrix. The performance of the constructed model is assessed using the Kappa Statistic, Sensitivity, Specificity, Prevalence, Balance Accuracy and Mcnemar's P measures. From the measures, it can be concluded that the model constructed in the study could be able to detect the frauds in credit cards with 70% accuracy level.

The proposed approach employed a variety of CNN models to extract deep features, which were then categorized using KNN and CNN classifiers, as described above. To evaluate the performance of the deep models, the outputs of the Stack ensemble models were used both individually and collectively to analyze their performance. According to the results, concatenated models outperformed independent models in the assessment. In addition, the KNN classifier outperformed the CNN classifier in terms of accuracy and precision. The best accuracy was achieved by the stack ensemble classifier, which achieved a score of 98.3 percent. We hope to be able to extract features from deep models in the future by using their convolution layers in the future. The implementation of feature selection techniques might aid in the selection of effective features for a given situation. Other types of classifiers will be investigated as well.

*****

7. Machine Learning for Detecting Abnormalities in Biomedical Data

Introduction

Machine learning tasks are typically classified into two broad categories, depending on whether there is a learning "label" or "feedback" available to a learning system: supervised learning and unsupervised learning (Park2018). Logistic regression is one of the most popular Machine Learning algorithms, which comes under the Supervised Learning technique. It is used for predicting the categorical dependent variable using a given set of independent variables. Logistic regression is a model that is used for binary classification, but it can be extended to do multiclass. The algorithm outputs a probability of the class, which can be useful. Examples of binary labels include: alive/dead, healthy/sick, or pass/fail (Medved2018). An ambitious visión of how machine learning could impact healthcare, outlining the progress and challenges of applying machine learning approaches to clinical diagnostics, precision therapeutics, and health monitoring (Goecks2020).

Data Description

There are 570 instances were used and the variables are radius (mean of distances from centre to points on the perimeter), texture (standard deviation of greyscale values), perimeter and area. The data has been collected from Kaggle.

Methodology

Machine learning is a sub-field of artificial intelligence (AI). The goal of machine learning generally is to understand the structure of data and fit that data into models that can be understood and utilized by people. In machine learning, tasks are generally classified into broad categories. These categories are based on how learning is received or how feedback on the learning is given to the system developed. Two of the most widely adopted machine learning methods are supervised learning which trains algorithms based on example input and output data that is labelled by humans, and unsupervised learning which provides the algorithm with no labelled data in order to allow it to find structure within its input data.

Logistic Regression

Logistic regression predicts the output of a categorical dependent variable. Therefore, the outcome must be a categorical or discrete value. It can be either Yes or No, 0 or 1, true or False, etc. but instead of giving the exact value as 0 and 1, it gives the probabilistic values which lie between 0 and 1. The Logistic regression equation can obtain from the Linear Regression equation. The mathematical steps to get Logistic Regression equation given below:

We know the general form of the equation of the straight line can be written as:

$$y = \beta_0 + b_1x_1 + b_2x_2 + b_3x_3 + \cdots + b_nx_n$$

Algorithm

Let t be a linear combination of the features xi and a set of weights wi, see above equation, where w0 is the intercept term.

$$t = w0 + w1x1 + \ldots + wixi,$$

where wi are the regression coefficients, indicating the relative effect of a particular feature on the outcome.

The logistic function σ , is defined by above equation and illustrated in Figure 7.1. This function is between 0 and 1 for every t. For positive infinity, it is equal to 1 and for negative it is 0 . It is therefore interpretable as a probability.

$$\sigma(t) = \frac{1}{1+e^{-t}}$$

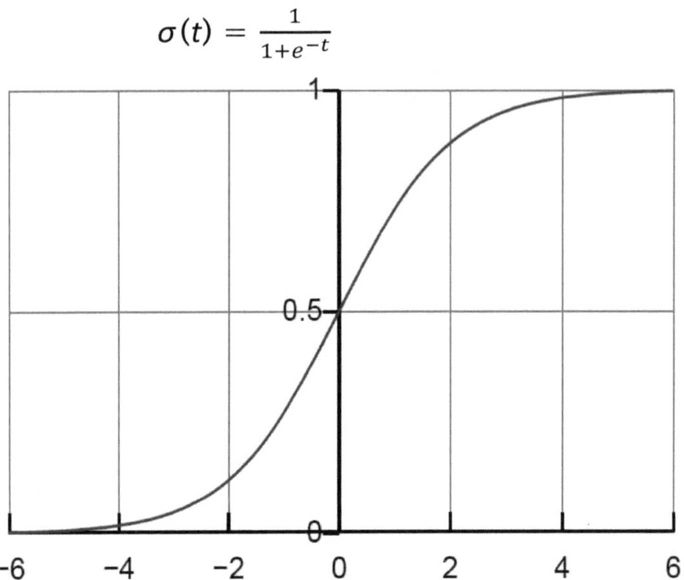

Figure 7.1: Graph of the logistic function

If we substitute t in above equation, we get equation,

$$\sigma(t) = \frac{1}{1 + e^{-(w0+w1x1+\ldots+wixi)}}$$

To go from a probability to a binary classification, we use a threshold k, which is often 0.5,

$$L(t,k) = \begin{cases} 1, & for\ \sigma(t) \geq k \\ 0, & for\ \sigma(t) \geq k \end{cases}$$

Fitting the model to the data means finding the weights wi that in some sense are optimal in predicting the observations. It is possible to solve this optimization problem using several different algorithms, using for example limited-memory Broyden-Fletcher-Goldfarb-Shanno (L-BFGS) or stochastic gradient descent (SGD) (Bottou2010; Byrd1995). Often some kind of regularization is used to reduce the possible overfit, see next paragraph for more information.

Regularization.

In order to minimize the possible overfit of a logistic regression model, regularization is often used. The basic idea is that an overly complex model often fits noise to the labels, thus will not generalize well to unseen data. To address this issue, a penalty term is added to the loss function, so that when we try to minimize the function we also try to minimize the model complexity, see the equation.

$$\min_{f} \sum L(y, f(x)) + \lambda R(f)$$

where L is a loss function that describes the cost of predicting f (x) when the label is y. λ controls the importance of the regularization term, R(f) which typically is a penalty on the complexity of f , usually a norm of model weights.

K-Nearest Neighbour

K-Nearest Neighbour is one of the simplest Machine Learning algorithms based on Supervised Learning technique. K-NN algorithm assumes the similarity between the new case/data and available cases and put the new case into the category that is most similar to the available categories. K-NN algorithm stores all the available data and classifies a new data point based on the similarity. This means when new data appears then it can be easily classified into a well suite category by using K- NN algorithm.

K-NN algorithm can be used for Regression as well as for Classification but mostly it is used for the Classification problems. K-NN is a non-parametric algorithm, which means it does not make any assumption on underlying data. It is also called a lazy learner algorithm because it does not learn from the training set immediately instead it stores the dataset and at the time of classification, it performs an action on the dataset. KNN algorithm at the training phase just stores the dataset and when it gets new data, then it classifies that data into a category that is much similar to the new data.

Support Vector Classifier

The most applicable machine-learning algorithm for our problem is Linear SVC. Before hopping into Linear SVC with our data, we're going to show a very simple example that should help solidify your understanding of working with Linear SVC. The objective of a Linear SVC (Support Vector Classifier) is to fit to the data you provide, returning a "best fit" hyperplane that divides, or categorizes, your data. From there, after getting the hyperplane, you can then feed some features to your classifier to see what the "predicted" class is.

Model Evaluation

The performance of each Machine Learning technique can be evaluated using various performance measures like Accuracy, Sensitivity, Specificity, and Precision (Shajahaan (2013)). These measures are defined by four decisions: True Positive (TP), True Negative (TN), False Positive (FN) and False Negative (FN). TP decision occurs when malignant instances predicted rightly.TN decision benign instances predicted rightly. FP decision occurs when benign instances predicted as malignant. FN decision occurs when malignant instances predicted as benign.

Accuracy can be calculated as Accuracy = $\frac{TP+TN}{TP+TN+FP+FN}$

Sensitivity can be calculated as Sensitivity= $\frac{TP}{TP+FN}$

Specificity can be calculated as Specificity= $\frac{TN}{TP+FP}$

Precision can calculate as Precision = $\frac{TP}{TP+FP}$

Result and Discussion

The heat map Figure 7.2 clearly shows that the attributes like mean perimeter to mean radius have positive correlation with the target attribute. Mean radius through mean area also have a high positive correlation (0.99). Diagnosis through mean perimeter and diagnosis through mean radius have highly negative correlation (-0.74 and -0.73).

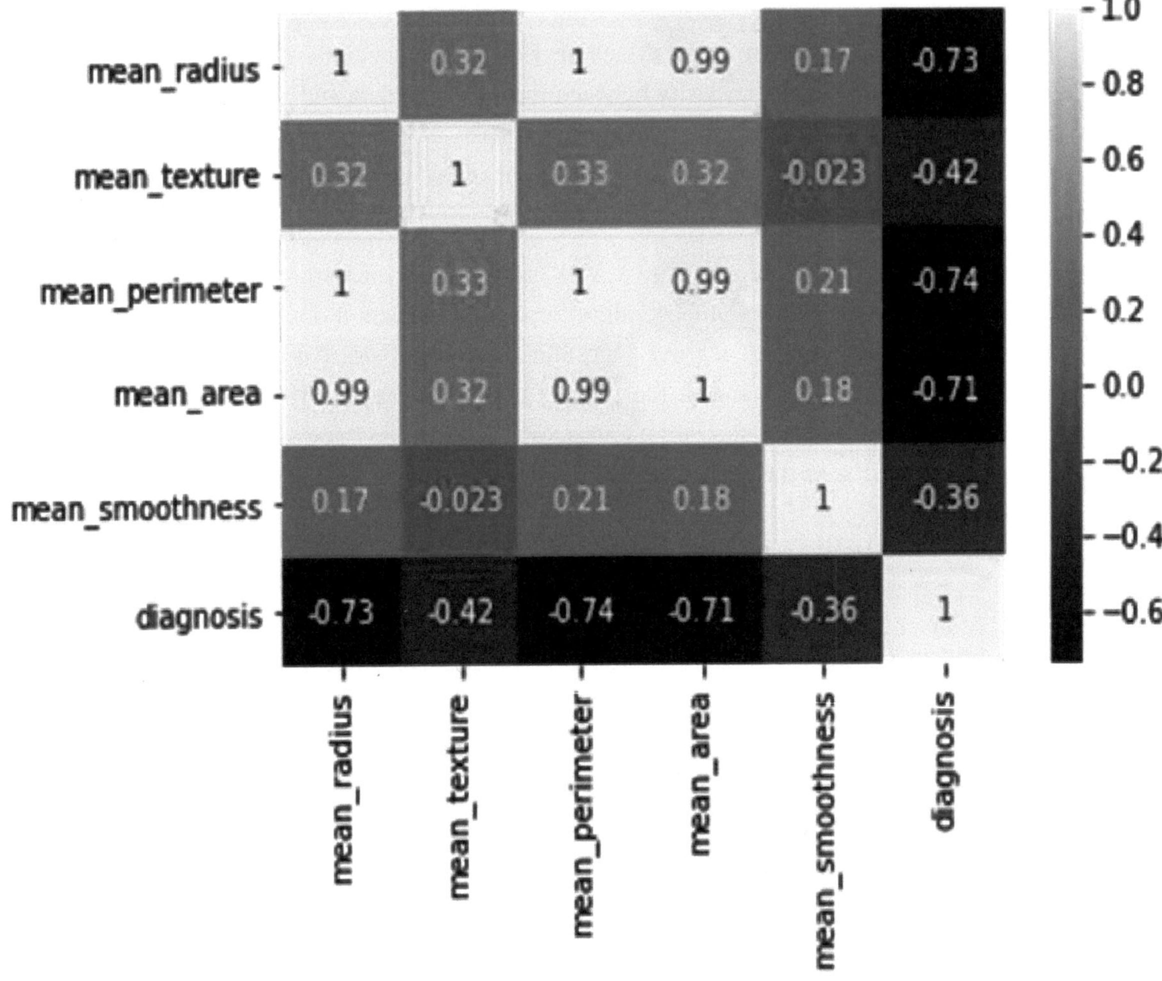

Figure 7.2: Heat Map for Breast Cancer data

The data set has divided into two parts, training data, which is 80% of the whole dataset, and testing data, which is 20% of the whole data set. After preparing the data, the algorithms are applied and the confusion matrix has found out. The accuracy has found out with the use of a confusion matrix.

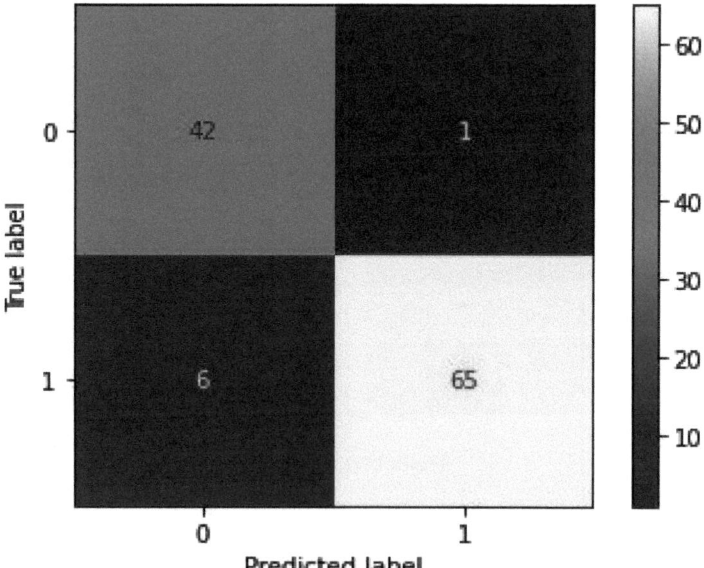

Figure 7.3: Confusion matrix for logistic model

Confusion matrix used to indicate the quality of the classifier for correct prediction. The count value in the confusion matrix Figure 7.4 shows the number of correct and incorrect classifier predictions using the logistic model. The top row of the confusion matrix gives the predicted positive events with true positive and bottom row corresponds to no events with true negatives. In other words, the diagonal elements represent the number of predicted target classes equal to the true target class. In addition, off diagonal elements correspond to the misclassified or incorrectly predicted target class. The accuracy score of logistic models is 0.94 (94%) have correctly classified.

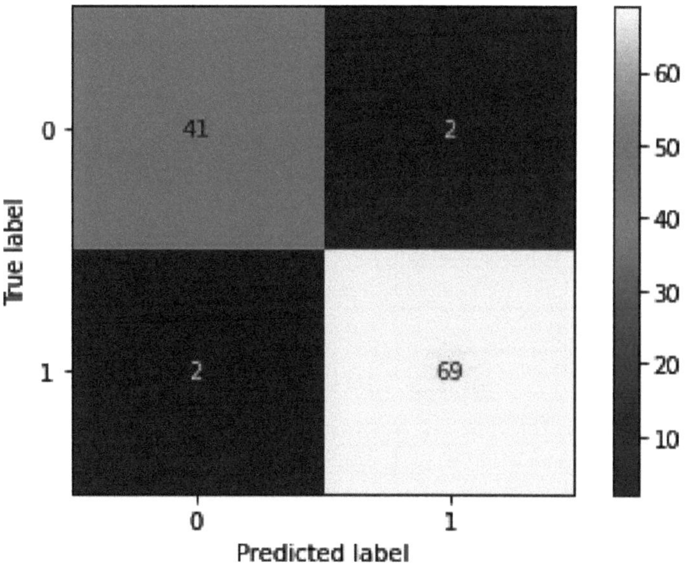

Figure 7.4: Confusion Matrix for KNN Model

The same data set used for classification using KNN model. Also using the algorithm, we selected different neighbors and implemented the KNN algorithm using optimum k value to get good result. The plot of confusion matrix given in Figure 6.4 for predicted classes against true classes and the accuracy level is 0.97 (97%).

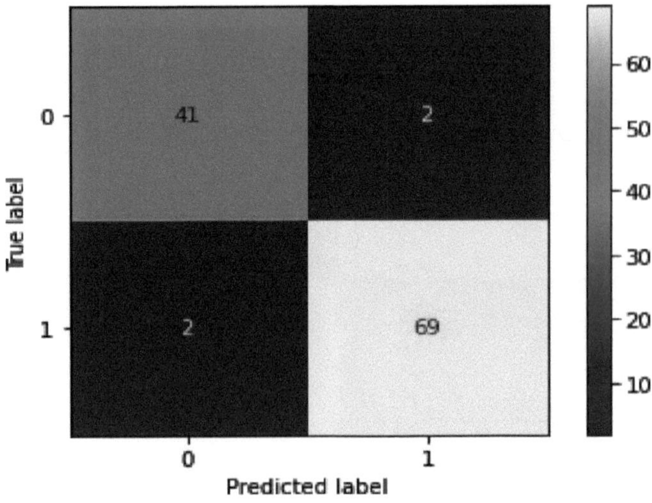

Figure 7.5: Confusion matrix for SVC model

The Figure 7.5 shows that the confusion matrix for SVC (Support Vector Classifier), the left upper box and right lower box represent the correctly predicted levels and others are wrongly predicted. The Model accuracy for SVC is 0.96 (96%). The Table 7.1 shows the results of the classification of the breast cancer data related to the diagnosis label in the issue report. Still, both of the proposed KNN and SVC models showed high F-score values compared to logistic model. Both KNN and SVC models showed 96% f1-score. While logistic model showed 94% f1-score. Compare to this three methods KNN and SVC model performed better for classifying breast cancer dataset.

Table 7.1: Classification report for Logistic, KNN, SVC models

Classification report					
		precision	Recall	F1 Score	Support
Logistic Model	0	0.88	0.98	0.92	43
	1	0.98	0.92	0.95	71
	accuracy			0.94	114
	macro avg.	0.93	0.95	0.94	114
	weighted avg.	0.94	0.94	0.94	114
		precision	Recall	F1 Score	Support
KNN Model	0	0.95	0.95	0.95	43
	1	0.97	0.97	0.97	71
	accuracy			0.96	114
	macro avg.	0.96	0.96	0.96	114
	weighted avg.	0.96	0.96	0.96	114
		precision	Recall	F1 Score	Support
SVC Model	0	0.95	0.95	0.95	43
	1	0.97	0.97	0.97	71
	accuracy			0.96	114
	macro avg.	0.96	0.96	0.96	114
	weighted avg.	0.96	0.96	0.96	114

\

AUC (Area under Curve) is ultimately a measure of the separation between classes in a binary classifier in the Figure 7.6 the blue and orange line is relatively close to the green one, which means that the classifier is good. With the ROC curve closer to the axes and the "elbow" close to the coordinate (0, 1).

The area under that line is 0.5, and the perfect ROC Curve would have an area of 1. As

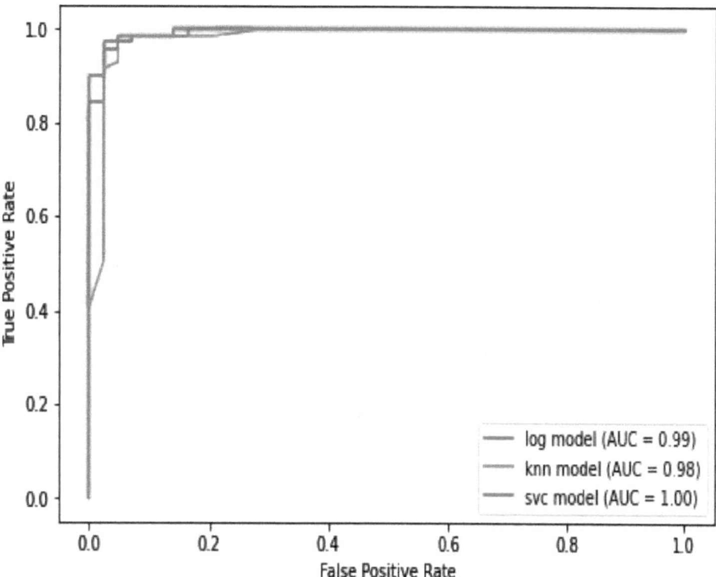

Figure 7.6: ROC AUC Curve for model performance

Closer as our model's ROC AUC is from 1, the better it is in separating classes and making better predictions. In this data, all the three models AUC values are closely one but log and SVC models values are nearly one high compared to KNN model.

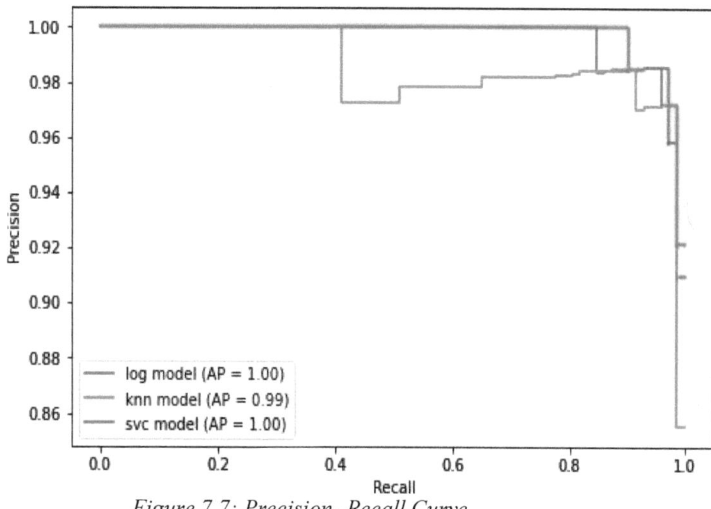

Figure 7.7: Precision- Recall Curve

The Precision-Recall Curve Fig.6 for the Logistic, KNN and SVC model showed. The Precision-Recall AUC is just like the ROC AUC, in that it summarizes the curve with a range of threshold values as a single score. The score can use as a point of comparison between different models on a binary classification problem where a score of 1.0 represents a model with perfect skill.in the breast cancer data log and SVC scores are exactly 1 and KNN score is closely one (0.99). Overall, the comparison of these three models (Logistic, KNN and SVC) Support Vector Classifier model will give the high accuracy; high precision recall score and ROC AUC coordinate value. So, this model will be useful for classify the breast cancer data and the prediction level very high.

Summary

In this chapter, we try to attempt on the breast cancer datasets considered to apply for machine learning Techniques. The radius, texture, perimeter, area of the tumour in 570 instances are the variables under the study. Logistic Regression, K-Nearest Neighbour Algorithm, and Support Vector Classifier is implemented. The Heat Map is generated to depict the correlation between the variables. The confusion matrix, precision, Recall, F1 score are the determination measures to check and compare the performance of Machine Learning Algorithms. The ROC-AUC Cure, Precision – Recall cure also fitted using the comparative measures. From the measures, it can be concluded that the Support Vector Classifier contains the better predication accuracy. The two important properties of the machine learning models such as relative accuracy and transferability to different genres without hindrances are demonstrated. Further, improvement in the potential of the machine learning models corresponding to the increase in the volume of training dataset and expansion of computational resources are also investigated. These studies are conducted with special reference to the problem of breast cancer detection.

References

1. Adewumi, Aderemi O and Akinyelu, Andronicus A (2017). "A survey of machine-learning and nature-inspired based credit card fraud detection techniques". In: International Journal of System Assurance Engineering and Management 8.2, pp. 937–953.

2. Agrawal, Prerna and Trivedi, Bhushan (2021). "Machine Learning Classifiers for Android Malware Detection". In: Data Management, Analytics and Innovation. Ed. by Neha Sharma et al. Singapore: Springer Singapore, pp. 311–322. ISBN: 978-981-15-5616-6.

3. Akila, S. and Reddy, U. Srinivasulu (2017). "Credit Card Fraud Detection Using Non-Overlapped Risk Based Bagging Ensemble (NRBE)". In: 2017 IEEE International Conference on Computational Intelligence and Computing Research (ICCIC), pp. 1–4.

4. Alam, Md. Noor et al. (2021). "Effective Machine Learning Approaches for Credit Card Fraud Detection". In: Innovations in Bio-Inspired Computing and Applications. Ed. by Ajith Abraham et al. Cham: Springer International Publishing, pp. 154–163. ISBN: 978-3-030-73603-3.

5. Aleskerov, E., Freisleben, B., and Rao, B. (1997). "CARDWATCH: a neural network-based database mining system for credit card fraud detection". In: Proceedings of the IEEE/IAFE 1997 Computational Intelligence for Financial Engineering (CIFEr), pp. 220–226.

6. Al-Shabi, Mohammed (Aug. 2019). "Credit Card Fraud Detection Using Autoencoder Model in Unbalanced Datasets". In: Journal of Advances in Mathematics and Computer Science, pp. 1–16.

7. Arora, Suman and Kumar, Dharminder (2017). "Selection of optimal credit card fraud detection models using a coefficient sum approach". In: 2017 International Conference on Computing, Communication and Automation (ICCCA), pp. 482–487.

8. Awoyemi, John O., Adetunmbi, Adebayo O., and Oluwadare, Samuel A. (2017). "Credit card fraud detection using machine learning techniques: A comparative analysis". In: 2017 International Conference on Computing Networking and Informatics (ICCNI), pp. 1–9.

9. Balasupramanian, N., Ephrem, Ben George, and Al-Barwani, Imad Salim (2017). "User pattern based online fraud detection and prevention using big data analytics and self-organizing maps". In: 2017 International Conference on Intelligent Computing, Instrumentation and Control Technologies (ICICICT), pp. 691–694.

10. Bin Sulaiman, Rejwan, Schetinin, Vitaly, and Sant, Paul (2022). "Review of Machine Learning Approach on Credit Card Fraud Detection". In: Human-Centric Intelligent Systems 2.1, pp. 55–68.

11. Bottou, Léon (2010). "Large-Scale Machine Learning with Stochastic Gradient Descent". In: Proceedings of COMPSTAT'2010. Ed. by Yves Lechevallier and Gilbert Saporta. Heidelberg: Physica-Verlag HD, pp. 177–186. ISBN: 978-3-7908-2604-3.

12. Boumaraf, Said et al. (2021). "Conventional Machine Learning versus Deep Learning for Magnification Dependent Histopathological Breast Cancer Image Classification: A Comparative Study with Visual Explanation". In: Diagnostics 11.3.

13. Brabazon, Anthony et al. (2010). "Identifying Online Credit Card Fraud using Artificial Immune Systems". In: pp. 1–7.

14. Brause, R., Langsdorf, T., and Hepp, M. (1999). "Neural data mining for credit card fraud detection". In: Proceedings 11th International Conference on Tools with Artificial Intelligence, pp. 103–106.

15. Byrd, Richard H. et al. (Sept. 1995). "A limited memory algorithm for bound constrained optimization". In: SIAM Journal of Scientific Computing 16, pp. 1190–1208.

16. Cai, Baoping, Huang, Lei, and Xie, Min (2017). "Bayesian Networks in Fault Diagnosis". In: IEEE Transactions on Industrial Informatics 13.5, pp. 2227–2240.

17. Carneiro, Nuno, Figueira, Gonçalo, and Costa, Miguel (2017). "A data mining based system for credit-card fraud detection in e-tail". In: Decision Support Systems 95, pp. 91–101.

18. Chen, Rongchang et al. (2005). "Novel questionnaire-responded transaction approach with SVM for credit card fraud detection". In: International Symposium on Neural Networks. Springer, pp. 916–921.

19. Chen, Rong-Chang, Chen, Taishi, and Lin, Chih-Chiang (Mar. 2006). "A new binary support vector system for increasing detection rate of credit card fraud". In: IJPRAI 20, pp. 227–239.

20. Choi, Rene Y. et al. (Feb. 2020). "Introduction to Machine Learning, Neural Networks and Deep Learning". In: Translational vision science & technology 9 (2), p. 14.

21. Chugh, Gunjan, Kumar, Shailender, and Singh, Nanhay (2021). "Survey on machine learning and deep learning applications in breast cancer diagnosis". In: Cognitive Computation 13.6, pp. 1451–1470.

22. Ciaburro, Giuseppe and Venkateswaran, Balaji (2017). "Neural Networks with R: Smart models using CNN, RNN, deep learning, and artificial intelligence principles". In.

23. Darwish, Saad M (2020a). "A bio-inspired credit card fraud detection model based on user behavior analysis suitable for business management in electronic banking". In: Journal of Ambient Intelligence and Humanized Computing 11.11, pp. 4873–4887.

24. Deshpande, Vijayshree B. Nipane; Poonam S. Kalinge; Dipali Vidhate; Kunal War; Bhagyashree P. (2016). "Fraudulent Detection in Credit Card SystemUsing SVM & Decision Tree". In: International Journal of Scientific Development and Research (IJSDR).

25. Dhankhad, Sahil, Mohammed, Emad, and Far, Behrouz (2018). "Supervised Machine Learning Algorithms for Credit Card Fraudulent Transaction Detection: A Comparative Study". In: 2018 IEEE International Conference on Information Reuse and Integration (IRI), pp. 122–125.

26. Dighe, Deepti, Patil, Sneha, and Kokate, Shrikant (2018). "Detection of Credit Card Fraud Transactions Using Machine Learning Algorithms and Neural Networks: A Comparative Study". In: 2018 Fourth International Conference on Computing Communication Control and Automation (ICCUBEA), pp. 1–6.

27. Dong, Weichuan et al. (Jan. 2022). "Phenotype Discovery and Geographic Disparities of Late-Stage Breast Cancer Diagnosis across U.S. Counties: A Machine Learning Approach." In: Cancer

epidemiology, biomarkers and prevention: a publication of the American Association for Cancer Research, cosponsored by the American Society of Preventive Oncology 31 (1), pp. 66–76.

28. Dornadula, Vaishnavi Nath and Geetha, S (2019). "Credit Card Fraud Detection using Machine Learning Algorithms". In: Procedia Computer Science 165. 2nd International Conference on Recent Trends in Advanced Computing ICRTAC -DISRUP - TIV INNOVATION, 2019 November 11-12, 2019, pp. 631–641.

29. Dubey, Saurabh C., Mundhe, Ketan S., and Kadam, Aditya A. (2020). "Credit Card Fraud Detection using Artificial Neural Network and BackPropagation". In: 2020 4th International Conference on Intelligent Computing and Control Systems (ICICCS), pp. 268–273.

30. Erb, Randall J. (1993). "Introduction to Backpropagation Neural Network Computation". In: Pharmaceutical Research 10.2, pp. 165–170.

31. Fu, Kang et al. (2016). "Credit Card Fraud Detection Using Convolutional Neural Networks". In: Neural Information Processing. Ed. by Akira Hirose et al. Cham: Springer International Publishing, pp. 483–490. ISBN: 978-3-319-46675-0.

32. Ghobadi, Fahimeh and Rohani, Mohsen (2016). "Cost sensitive modeling of credit card fraud using neural network strategy". In: 2016 2nd international conference of signal processing and intelligent systems (ICSPIS). IEEE, pp. 1–5.

33. Ghosh and Reilly (1994). "Credit card fraud detection with a neural-network". In: 1994 Proceedings of the Twenty-Seventh Hawaii International Conference on System Sciences. Vol. 3, pp. 621–630.

34. Goecks, Jeremy et al. (Apr. 2020). "How Machine Learning Will Transform Biomedicine." In: Cell 181 (1), pp. 92–101.

35. Goyal, Rahul and Manjhvar, Amit Kumar (2020). "Review on Credit Card Fraud Detection using Data Mining Classification Techniques & Machine Learning Algorithms". In: IJRAR-International Journal of Research and Analytical Reviews (IJRAR), E-ISSN, pp. 2348–1269.

36. Hamzah Ali Shukur, Sefer Kurnaz (2019). "Credit Card Fraud Detection using Machine Learning Methodology". In: International Journal of Computer Science and Mobile Computing (IJCSMC).

37. Han, Jiawei, Pei, Jian, and Tong, Hanghang (2022). Data mining: concepts and techniques. Morgan kaufmann.

38. Hochreiter, Sepp and Schmidhuber, Jürgen (Nov. 1997). "Long Short-Term Memory". In: Neural Computation 9.8, pp. 1735–1780. eprint: https://direct.mit. edu/neco/article-pdf/9/8/1735/813796/neco.1997.9.8.1735.pdf.

39. Husejinovic, Admel (Jan. 2020). "Credit card fraud detection using naive Bayesian and C4.5 decision tree classifiers". In: 8, pp. 1–5.

40. Jha, Sanjeev, Guillen, Montserrat, and Westland, J. (Nov. 2012). "Employing transaction aggregation strategy to detect credit card fraud". In: Expert Systems with Applications 39, pp. 12650–12657.

41. Jiang, Changjun et al. (Mar. 2018). "Credit Card Fraud Detection: A Novel Approach Using Aggregation Strategy and Feedback Mechanism". In: IEEE Internet of Things Journal PP.5, pp. 1–1.

42. Jurgovsky, Johannes et al. (2018). "Sequence classification for credit-card fraud detection". In: Expert Systems with Applications 100, pp. 234–245.

43. Kazemi, Zahra and Zarrabi, Houman (2017). "Using deep networks for fraud detection in the credit card transactions". In: 2017 IEEE 4th International Conference on Knowledge-Based Engineering and Innovation (KBEI), pp. 0630–0633.

44. Khatun, Tania et al. (2021). "Performance Analysis of Breast Cancer: A Machine Learning Approach". In: 2021 Third International Conference on Inventive Research in Computing Applications (ICIRCA). IEEE, pp. 1426–1434.

45. Kohavi, Ron and Provost, Foster (1998). "Glossary of terms journal of machine learning". In: Mach. Learn

46. Krenker, Andrej et al. (Feb. 2009). "Bidirectional Artificial Neural Networks for Mobile-Phone Fraud Detection". In: ETRI Journal 31.

47. Kumar, M. Suresh et al. (2019). "Credit Card Fraud Detection Using Random Forest Algorithm". In: 2019 3rd International Conference on Computing and Communications Technologies (ICCCT), pp. 149–153.

48. Lebichot, Bertrand et al. (2017). "A graph-based, semi-supervised, credit card fraud detection system". In: Complex Networks & Their Applications V. Ed. by Hocine Cherifi et al. Cham: Springer International Publishing, pp. 721–733. ISBN: 978-3-319-50901-3.

49. Li, Chenglong et al. (Jan. 2021). "Application of Credit Card Fraud Detection Based on CS-SVM". In: International Journal of Machine Learning and Computing 11, pp. 34–39.

50. Li, Zhenchuan et al. (2018). "Credit Card Fraud Detection via Kernel-Based Supervised Hashing". In: pp. 1249–1254.

51. Lu, Qibei and Ju, Chun-hua (2011). "Research on Credit Card Fraud Detection Model Based on Class Weighted Support Vector Machine". In: Journal of Convergence Information Technology 6, pp. 62–68.

52. Majhi, Soumen et al. (2019). "Chimera states in neuronal networks: a review". In: Physics of life reviews 28, pp. 100–121.

53. Makki, Sara et al. (2019). "An Experimental Study with Imbalanced Classification Approaches for Credit Card Fraud Detection". In: IEEE Access 7, pp. 93010–93022.

54. Manoj, K (July 2015). "Outlier detection in datamining". PhD thesis. Manonmaniam Sundaranar University.

55. Medved, Dennis (2018). "Deep Learning Applications for Biomedical Data and Natural Language Processing". Defence details Date: 2018-09-17 Time: 13:00 Place: lecture hall E:1406, building E, Ole Römers väg 3, Lund University, Faculty of Engineering LTH, Lund External reviewer(s) Name: Lisboa, Paul Title: Professor Affiliation: Liverpool John Moores University, UK —. PhD thesis. Department of Computer Science. ISBN: 978-91-7753-792-2.

56. Modi, Krishna (Aug. 2017). "Fraud Detection Technique in Credit Card Transactions using Convolutional Neural Network". In: International Journal of Advance Research in Engineering, Science & Technology 4, pp. 2394–2444.

57. Modi, Krishna and Dayma, Reshma (2017). "Review on fraud detection methods in credit card transactions". In: 2017 International Conference on Intelligent Computing and Control (I2C2). IEEE, pp. 1–5.

58. Moody, John and Darken, Christian J. (June 1989). "Fast Learning in Networks of Locally-Tuned Processing Units". In: Neural Computation 1.2, pp. 281–294.

59. Najadat, Hassan et al. (2020). "Credit Card Fraud Detection Based on Machine and Deep Learning". In: 2020 11th International Conference on Information and Communication Systems (ICICS), pp. 204–208.

60. Nielsen, Michael A (2015). Neural networks and deep learning. Vol. 25. Determination press San Francisco, CA, USA.

61. Ogwueleka, Francisca (June 2011). "Data mining application in credit card fraud detection system". In: Journal of Engineering Science and Technology 6, pp. 311–322.

62. Olowookere, Toluwase Ayobami and Adewale, Olumide Sunday (2020). "A framework for detecting credit card fraud with cost-sensitive meta-learning ensemble approach". In: Scientific African 8, e00464.

63. Ostapowicz, Michał and Zbikowski, Kamil (Oct. 2019). "Detecting Fraudulent Accounts on Blockchain: A Supervised Approach". In: pp. 18–31. ISBN: 978-3-030-34222-7.

64. Park, Cheolsoo, Took, Clive Cheong, and Seong, Joon-Kyung (Feb. 2018). "Machine learning in biomedical engineering." In: Biomedical engineering letters. Vol. 8. Germany, pp. 1–3.

65. Patidar, Raghavendra, Sharma, Lokesh, et al. (2011). "Credit card fraud detection using neural network". In: International Journal of Soft Computing and Engineering (IJSCE) 1.32-38.

66. Pojee, Dastgir et al. (2017). "Secure and quick NFC payment with data mining and intelligent fraud detection". In: 2017 2nd International Conference on Communication and Electronics Systems (ICCES), pp. 148–152.

67. Pozzolo, Andrea Dal and Bontempi, Gianluca (2015). "Adaptive Machine Learning for Credit Card Fraud Detection". In.

68. Prusti, Debachudamani and Rath, Santanu Kumar (2019). "Web service-based credit card fraud detection by applying machine learning techniques". In: TENCON 2019 - 2019 IEEE Region 10 Conference (TENCON), pp. 492–497.

69. Quah, Jon T.S. and Sriganesh, M. (2008). "Real-time credit card fraud detection using computational intelligence". In: Expert Systems with Applications 35.4, pp. 1721–1732

70. Rai, Arun Kumar and Dwivedi, Rajendra Kumar (2020). "Fraud Detection in Credit Card Data using Unsupervised Machine Learning Based Scheme". In: 2020 International Conference on Electronics and Sustainable Communication Systems (ICESC), pp. 421–426.

71. Randhawa, Kuldeep et al. (2018). "Credit Card Fraud Detection Using AdaBoost and Majority Voting". In: IEEE Access 6, pp. 14277–14284.

72. Roy, Abhimanyu et al. (2018). "Deep learning detecting fraud in credit card transactions". In: 2018 Systems and Information Engineering Design Symposium (SIEDS), pp. 129–134.

73. Rtayli, Naoufal and Enneya, Nourddine (2020). "Selection Features and Support Vector Machine for Credit Card Risk Identification". In: Procedia Manufacturing 46. 13th International Conference Interdisciplinarity in Engineering, INTER-ENG 2019, 3–4 October 2019, Targu Mures, Romania, pp. 941–948.

74. Sahin, Yusuf and Duman, Ekrem (2011). "Detecting credit card fraud by decision trees and support vector machines". In: Proceedings of the International MultiConference of Engineers and Computer Scientists. Newswood Limited, pp. 442–447.

75. Samuel, Arthur L (1988). "Some studies in machine learning using the game of checkers. II - recent progress". In: Computer Games I, pp. 366–400.

76. Saraswathi, R Vijaya et al. (2021). "Leaf disease detection and remedy suggestion using convolutional neural networks". In: 2021 5th International Conference on Computing Methodologies and Communication (ICCMC). IEEE, pp. 788–794.

77. Sasank, JVV Sriram et al. (2019). "Credit Card Fraud Detection Using Various Classification and Sampling Techniques: A Comparative Study". In: 2019 International Conference on Communication and Electronics Systems (ICCES). IEEE, pp. 1713–1718.

78. Save, Prajal et al. (Mar. 2017). "A Novel Idea for Credit Card Fraud Detection using Decision Tree". In: International Journal of Computer Applications 161, pp. 6–9.

79. Saxena, Shweta, Shukla, Sanyam, and Gyanchandani, Manasi (Sept. 2020). "Pre-trained convolutional neural networks as feature extractors for diagnosis of breast cancer using histopathology". In: International Journal of Imaging Systems and Technology 30.

80. Shahin, Muhammad A and Symons, Stephen J (2011). "Detection of Fusarium damaged kernels in Canada Western Red Spring wheat using visible/near-infrared hyperspectral imaging and principal component analysis". In: Computers and electronics in agriculture 75.1, pp. 107–112.

81. Shalev-Shwartz, Shai and Ben-David, Shai (2014). Understanding Machine Learning: From Theory to Algorithms. USA: Cambridge University Press. ISBN: 1107057132.

82. Sidey-Gibbons, Chris et al. (2021). "Development of machine learning algorithms for the prediction of financial toxicity in localized breast cancer following surgical treatment". In: JCO clinical cancer informatics 5, pp. 338–347.

83. Sohony, Ishan, Pratap, Rameshwar, and Nambiar, Ullas (2018). "Ensemble Learning for Credit Card Fraud Detection". In: Proceedings of the ACM India Joint International Conference on Data Science and Management of Data. CoDS-COMAD '18. Goa, India: Association for Computing Machinery, pp. 289–294. ISBN: 9781450363419.

84. Soni, Kartik M, Gupta, Amisha, and Jain, Tarun (2021). "Supervised Machine Learning Approaches for Breast Cancer Classification and a high performance Recurrent Neural Network". In: 2021 Third International Conference on Inventive Research in Computing Applications (ICIRCA). IEEE, pp. 1–7.

85. Srivastava, Abhinav et al. (2008). "Credit card fraud detection using hidden Markov model". In: IEEE Transactions on dependable and secure computing 5.1, pp. 37–48.

86. Suryanarayana, S Venkata, Balaji, GN, and Rao, G Venkateswara (2018). "Machine learning approaches for credit card fraud detection". In: Int. J. Eng. Technol 7.2, pp. 917–920.

87. Syeda, Mubeena, Zhang, Yan-Qing, and Pan, Yi (2002). "Parallel granular neural networks for fast credit card fraud detection". In: 2002 IEEE World Congress on Computational Intelligence. 2002 IEEE International Conference on Fuzzy Systems. FUZZ-IEEE'02. Proceedings (Cat. No. 02CH37291). Vol. 1. IEEE, pp. 572–577.

88. Taha, Altyeb Altaher and Malebary, Sharaf Jameel (2020). "An Intelligent Approach to Credit Card Fraud Detection Using an Optimized Light Gradient Boosting Machine". In: IEEE Access 8, pp. 25579–25587.

89. Thennakoon, Anuruddha et al. (July 2019). "Real-time Credit Card Fraud Detection Using Machine Learning". In.

90. Tran, Phuong Hanh et al. (2018). "Real Time Data-Driven Approaches for Credit Card Fraud Detection". In: Proceedings of the 2018 International Conference on E-Business and Applications. ICEBA 2018. Da Nang, Viet Nam: Association for Computing Machinery, pp. 6–9. ISBN: 9781450363686.

91. Tripathi, Diwakar et al. (2018). "Credit scoring model based on weighted voting and cluster based feature selection". In: Procedia computer science 132, pp. 22–31.

92. Uddin, Shahadat et al. (2019). "Comparing different supervised machine learning algorithms for disease prediction". In: BMC Medical Informatics and Decision Making 19.1, p. 281.

93. Vynokurova, Olena et al. (2020). "Hybrid Machine Learning System for Solving Fraud Detection Tasks". In: 2020 IEEE Third International Conference on Data Stream Mining and Processing (DSMP), pp. 1–5.

94. Wang, Chunzhi et al. (2018). "Credit Card Fraud Detection Based on Whale Algorithm Optimized BP Neural Network". In: 2018 13th International Conference on Computer Science & Education (ICCSE), pp. 1–4.

95. Wen, Hanlin and Huang, Fangming (2020). "Personal Loan Fraud Detection Based on Hybrid Supervised and Unsupervised Learning". In: pp. 339–343.

96. Whitrow, C. et al. (Feb. 2009). "Transaction aggregation as a strategy for credit card fraud detection". In: Data Mining and Knowledge Discovery 18, pp. 30–55.

97. Wiese, Bénard and Omlin, Christian (2009). "Credit Card Transactions, Fraud Detection, and Machine Learning: Modelling Time with LSTM Recurrent Neural Networks". In: Innovations in Neural Information Paradigms and Applications. Ed. by Monica Bianchini et al. Berlin, Heidelberg: Springer Berlin Heidelberg, pp. 231–268. ISBN: 978-3-642-04003-0.

98. Xuan, Shiyang et al. (2018). "Random forest for credit card fraud detection". In: 2018 IEEE 15th International Conference on Networking, Sensing and Control (ICNSC), pp. 1–6.

99. Yang, Hsiao-Yu et al. (2021). "Breath biopsy of breast cancer using sensor array signals and machine learning analysis". In: Scientific Reports 11.1, pp. 1–9.

******

9 798890 661029

Printed by Libri Plureos GmbH in Hamburg,
Germany